GUERRILLA GARDENING

HOW TO CREATE GORGEOUS GARDENS FOR FREE

BARBARA PALLENBERG

ILLUSTRATIONS BY CATHY PAVIA

PHOTOGRAPHS BY LOU GAINES

RENAISSANCE BOOKS
Los Angeles

Library of Congress Control Number: 2001087570
ISBN: 1-58063-183-5

10 9 8 7 6 5 4 3 2 1

Design by Lisa-Theresa Lenthall
Typesetting by Jesús Arellano

Published by Renaissance Books
Distributed by St. Martin's Press
Manufactured in the United States of America
First edition

GUERRILLA GARDENING

For Ella Kate VRO—may she follow in my muddy footsteps

ACKNOWLEDGMENTS

None of this would have happened without Lindsay Maracotta, who heard me mumbling one day about my "guerrilla gardening" and said, "Write a book!" And then she put me together with all of the people who made it happen—Arthur Morey and Amanda Pisani, my editors; Lisa Lenthall and Jesús Arellano, my designers.

CONTENTS

It is the entrance to a flea market. No charge. Admittance free. . . .
I'm checking on what's in the world. What's left. What's discarded.
What's no longer cherished. What had to be sacrificed . . . there
might be something valuable, there. Not valuable, exactly. But
something I would want. Want to rescue. Something that speaks
to me. To my longings. . . .

—Susan Sontag, "The Volcano Lover"

HOW I BECAME A GUERRILLA GARDENER

It all started when I was in college. My roommate and I had a fabulous studio behind a broken-down bungalow. It was one huge, high-ceilinged room, with a brick patio through French doors out back, shaded by an old fig tree that we accessed for its fruit by climbing on the rotting roof of the garage. (The occasional Maserati or Ferrari my father sent to me from Italy—to sell, not drive—was parked outside the garage because of the rotting roof. It was a near-slum, that area, but in the late fifties no one knew what those cars were, and they were perfectly safe.) Anyway, that year I gained ten pounds eating figs— straight from the tree, fig bread, you name it.

At night we used to prowl around the grounds of the huge old mansions nearby, a few still maintained, most of them rooming houses. One, we discovered, had become a convent. It had a wonderful turn-of-the-century greenhouse full of exotic succulents. We decided we particularly liked one, very portable plant.

I don't know what happened to it as I graduated mid-year and Sue (still my close friend) closed down the place herself. I'll have to ask her—I know she took the dog back to New Orleans with her, in her little turquoise and white Nash Rambler. Maybe the plant, or its offspring, is still alive, somewhere.

Having sort of caught the spirit, we did a reconnaissance of a famous public garden soon after, which had a major collection of cactus and succulents, with the idea that we'd add to our plunder. We brought very large purses, went on a weekday when (in those times) we practically had the place to ourselves, and we "borrowed" cuttings from our favorite plants. I don't know what happened to those, either.

I went back to New York: apartments, scrambling, dating, working; a measly plant once in a while, flowers from some guy, years later when it became a food fashion, a basil plant which died when you went on vacation.

Fan palm near curb, on empty lot.

And then, a family and a house in southern California. And a dog, a pool, an orange tree—three requirements of Big Guy (he's the long-suffering unbelievably moral, ethical, truthful husband who quakes at the mere thought of . . .). And an acre of living things on a hillside. Not enough money (at least at first) to hire a gardener. Things died—age, gophers, disease, no fertilizer. So it began.

WHAT IS GUERRILLA GARDENING?

This manual is a compendium of information gathered from numerous sources (many of whom insist on anonymity, for reasons that will become clear), as well as my own lengthy experience on the front.

It is to be consulted responsibly (i.e., read between the lines) and not misused. It is not for children other than those under adult supervision, if you don't mind the moral ambiguity you are imparting. No responsibility is implied by this book in the event that users are involved in altercations with the law or property owners (who probably have a legitimate beef). The politically correct should remember that guerrilla gardeners are engaged in reclamation. We are saving the environment, cutting by cutting.

The information contained herein is for the rank-and-file foot soldier who is always on the front lines. Men and women of rank and position, who are able to delegate to others (gardeners), will find it of little use, unless they like to get down and dirty once in a while.

Within these pages you will learn how to design your own plan of attack and to clarify the purpose of your mission. You will be instructed on protective behavior and psychological and ecological warfare.

I have a friend who is fiercely independent, an ex-Warhol superstar, movie actress, painter, writer, et cetera. She doesn't like anything that grows, including children. Nonetheless, she noted, "If you're taking seeds and planting them elsewhere, who knows, maybe it's you who's saving the species from dying out. What if a botanical garden gets gang-raped? What if The Rare Plant Department contracts a cross-species virus, like ebola or mad cow disease? Maybe you, with your isolated little garden, will save the world."

After a long day in the trenches, the author relaxes at home.

This field manual will teach you how to identify plants for your garden that are able to grow from part of the original plant, or are easily uprooted from their present location and will be hearty enough to survive the move. Most importantly, the plants cost nothing.

It will also instruct you on where to find these flora legally, vaguely legally, and . . . gardener discretion is advised. You'll learn how to retrieve the plants: what weapons you'll need and helpful diversionary behavior. You'll also get examples of historical precedent and ecological rationale to use when you're caught defending your behavior to politically correct friends. This field manual is not meant to be exhaustive, because my aim is to give new recruits some basic training. Nor am I going to get into complicated propagation like grafting, because that's not a necessary skill for the typical foot soldier. If what is learned here leads the individual in that direction, fine and good luck.

A friend from Sotheby's was supervising the pickup of a large, valuable outdoor sculpture; the owner was nearly hysterical with worry that it would be dropped. The sculpture was fine, but the movers managed to snap off a huge branch of a jade plant as they struggled. My friend quickly hid the branch in a trash can and rubbed some dirt on the blazingly white exposed wound to give it a "patina." The owner didn't seem to notice. Later that night, however, my friend started thinking about the jade branch. He went back (in that neighborhood, all the trash cans are hidden in back alleys that are fenced off from the houses themselves) and retrieved the branch. It's now planted in his front yard.

To boost your morale, and to put the queasy among you at ease, I have included within this manual anecdotal information about this secret war. I can honestly report that an informal census has shown that among the gardening population of this country, one in four has served, unheralded, in this ongoing covert operation. I am sure the numbers are much larger in England, that hotbed of obsessive gardening. And who knows about the rest of the world, with the possible exception of the Arctic, where it's not worth the trouble, and the tropics, where it would be gilding the lily, so to speak.

CHAPTER ONE

A HISTORY OF CREATIVE CULTIVATION

Guerrilla gardening isn't a new phenomenon. If you need a bit of historical backup for your penurious little acts, there's plenty. After all, if native flora were never transported from one place to another, the huge variety we have come to expect in our landscapes, both cultivated and wild, would be nonexistent. It's happened to cuisines, viruses, and the human race, why not plants?

In fact, buying plants and trees is a relatively new phenomenon; it began around two hundred years ago, when growing from seed became a business. Before that, we all propagated our own, and since then, we have been discouraged by the "experts," who tell us to leave it to them. In the last ten or fifteen years, however, there's been a reaction against this kind of thinking—we don't trust the experts like we used to. Witness home breweries, alternative medicine, farmers' markets, self-help on the 'Net, and the like.

Not long after we stopped being hunter-gatherers and became farmers, someone noticed that when the branches of two trees rubbed against each other, injuring the bark and enabling the growing layers to contact, they would eventually join together. Thus propagation by grafting was born.

The first recorded reconnaissance of greenery was in 1495 B.C., when Egyptian Queen Hatshepsut brought back from what is now Somalia some young trees for their fragrant resin. It was probably the variety of tree, which still exists, that produces frankincense and myrrh.

The ancient Greeks planted cuttings and even used honey or milk or manure on them to make them root.

The Romans, major explorer-conquerors, brought their foliage to far-off lands; medieval monks, also intrepid travelers, gathered medicinal herbs wherever they went. The introduction of new plant life, however, really took off in the great colonization

A gorgeous old fig tree on an abandoned lot—no one ever takes the ripe fruit except me.

periods of the sixteenth–nineteenth centuries, when conquering countries—Spain, Germany, Holland, France, and especially England—brought back plants from their colonies in the Americas, Africa, India, the East Indies, the Orient, and Australia. We all know—right?—that the potato didn't spring up in Ireland (Peru), that tomatoes (from colonized America) were thought to be poison by Europeans, that there was no tobacco addiction till the plant was brought to England from Virginia. (Although I think I recently read somewhere that tobacco was found in a mummy's tomb . . . whatever.)

We'd have no morning o.j. if someone didn't take oranges out of China (remember those indoor-outdoor rooms in French and English castles called orangeries?). We'd have no rice for our chow mein, or our risotto. No bananas. *No kiwis.*

It was often an advance guard of missionaries and traders who first brought back exotic new plant life; then aristocratic amateur botanists started making forays, and finally, professional plant collectors were hired to do the job, by syndicates, nurseries, and private subscribers.

The young scion of a famous English publishing house told me that his entire family quaked when his grandmother returned from trips abroad. It's illegal to bring foreign plant life into England and she had a habit of stashing cuttings in her luggage from wherever her travels took her. He said she never got stopped—they figured it was probably because her imperious manner terrified the customs officials.

In the nineteenth century, pioneer brides took roses westward in their wagons, even sharing their drinking water to keep them alive. These old varieties, called heritage roses, are supported by numerous public and private gardens and rosarian societies around the country. There are little old ladies traveling on back roads all over looking for, and saving, lost roses at abandoned farms and cemeteries. And the world's biggest rosebush, according to the *Guinness Book of World Records,* was grown from a rooted cutting given by one pioneer woman to another 114 years ago in Tombstone, Arizona. By the way, my sister in Oklahoma has a plant from this rosebush—they sell cuttings, which is a great idea; the mama plant will never die.

To this day professionals and plant lovers scour remote corners of the globe—like 16,000 feet up in the Himalayas—looking for undiscovered plants. Gardening histories frequently write about heroes of the plant world, like those who saved rare plants from obliteration by taking cuttings from public gardens that subsequently lost their specimens to some tragedy. So you can just call yourself a freelance, self-employed plant explorer/collector if you're ambushed in the field, have an odd moment of self-doubt, or are attacked by a more conventional gardener at a cocktail party.

The only friend who didn't have a positive response to the notion of this book is a well-known novelist who writes garden articles for the New York Times; *she also has a beautiful garden in Westchester County. She said, "I'm the person who pores over catalogues of rare plant seeds and bulbs, buys them at enormous cost, plants them, and obsesses over them. I would be very unhappy if someone came along and snipped or uprooted something." I tried to reassure her that I was instructing my readers that beloved private gardens were never to be touched, that it would be like kidnapping, but that didn't calm her down. She told me about the PCers who point out that plant thieves damage the ecology by uprooting rare plants, and that they shouldn't even gather seeds. I gave up—there's one in every crowd.*

And if you need further ammunition, you can say that people like you are waging a secret and lonely war. But for your efforts, many old forms of plant life would be extinct—bred out of existence—were they not found in the gardens of those who have passed along cuttings from generation to generation. They're now called heirlooms, and there's a growing interest in this field by those very same politically correct gardeners, who pay lots for their heirloom seeds and bulbs. There have been countless news stories about the loss of biodiversity in our agricultural crops and garden plants, which are bred and now even genetically engineered to resist disease, withstand harsh conditions, and so on, and so on: you, dear soldier, are on the front lines defending against this foolhardiness. That ought to shut them up.

A movie producer I met, who used to be a journalist, was on the Golan Heights during the October War in 1973. He was staying off and on at a kibbutz near the front, and while there he met a police officer from whom he wanted to get some information. She was beautiful, and he told me he was (coincidentally) charmed by her. He wanted to give her something, but there was nothing to buy. So the night of a party attended by many police officers, he went to the settlement's garden and gathered a huge bunch of flowers and presented them to her. She was not charmed herself, as she knew exactly where they came from. He nearly got arrested; he lost the girl and didn't get the story.

If you're compulsively law-abiding, you can still indulge in a little warfare. The branches of your neighbor's tree that arch over your sun-starved flowers—you're perfectly within your rights to cut them back, thereby acquiring a nice selection of cuttings. Your neighbor, however, can sue you if you trim so much that you kill the tree. (And by the way, he does not have the right to amputate these marauding limbs—then you can sue him, for trespassing.) The same goes for acquisition in easements that cross common property lines. You can do further research in this area by checking local statutes.

CHAPTER TWO

BATTLE PLAN

Maybe you'd just like to see a few plants survive in your apartment window, which looks out onto a gloomy airshaft. Or maybe you have a little garden area in front of your rental and you'd like to get rid of the bare dirt and dead grass its former tenants considered a garden. Or, like a friend of mine in Colorado, your whole garden may consist of a long skinny plot on the side of your house, going back hundreds of feet. Maybe you're frantic because you have a 10,000-acre ranch and you have to do something about the area around the hacienda. Anyway: all of these recruits, even the apartment dweller, would do well to have a plan.

A very rich man I know planted exotic pear trees around his oceanfront house, and when they started to wither he had to install misting machines to keep the salt air off the leaves. Lesson: remember your climate when guerrilla gardening.

LAYING OUT YOUR CAMP

Assess the idiosyncrasies of your microclimate (i.e., no sun, warm year-round for Mr. Cliff Dweller), then start looking at what plants grow in your neighborhood (or your friend's equally gloomy apartment). If you want flowers or vegetables you'll have to think twice about trees. Trees make shade, which flowers and vegetables don't like. If your plot is essentially shade-bound, shade-loving plants should be your top priority. There are flowering ones and some with brilliant, unusually colored leaves. If you live where there are really cold winters, plant only what grows naturally in your climate, unless you're doing it all indoors. If you live in a really humid place, like a bayou, forget about desert plants, and so on.

One note of real importance: do not continue reading this book if all you want is a lawn. Guerrilla gardeners are antilawn, because:

- Lawns are boring.
- Lawns are environmentally hazardous (the nitrogen fertilizer and weed killers poured on lawns cause horrible imbalances when they eventually reach our oceans, and they cause illness and birth defects in humans and animals alike).
- Lawns are expensive to maintain.
- Those damn mowers woke me up this morning at 7:00 A.M.

Big Guy absolutely detests lawns because, first, he was made to mow his English grandparents' lawn when he stayed with them every summer (no power mowers back then) and second, he is at heart a lazy Roman. The other night we went to the movies with our neighbor (and before that a longtime friend). He told her that every time he looks down on her lawn from our deck he wants to throw up. She took it gracefully.

So, look around and see what you like. Find out if it takes a long time to grow and fill in bare spots, how long it lives, and how big it gets. I often take a twig to a local nursery to ask questions like these (and also "Is it poisonous?"—after my baby grand-daughter ate some Indian hawthorn berries). You'll find this kind of information on some of the more common and easy-to-grow plant life I've listed in chapter 4, Field Manual.

Then make an actual plan of your weed patch—it can be approximate—and fiddle around on paper with various layouts and combinations of plants (you can even do this on the com-puter—whatever it takes). In planning your garden-to-be, keep the following questions in mind:

- How easily does a plant take to propagation?
- Does the plant have flowers? If so, what color are they?
- What are the particular plant's environmental needs?
- Does it need a lot of water, or a little?
- What kind of soil does it do best in?
- Does it need to be in a warm climate?
- Does it need full sun, partial sun, or does it like the shade?
- Is the plant an annual? An annual will have to be replanted every year.
- If it's a tree, is it deciduous? Even in warmer climates some trees lose their leaves.

Of course, all of this research happens in an ideal world. What you'll probably use is my old fallback—trial and error. If you find that you don't care for the site you've selected, you can always move a propagated plant once it matures.

By planting the same plants together in a particular section of the garden, you can control the plants' environment more eas-ily. Generally, this type of arrangement will also have a planned appearance without looking formal and stiff. In my front yard, which is pretty small, I made a narrow, meandering dirt path that divides the garden into four areas. In one, I grow rosemary and lavender (both need a little water and a fair amount of sun). In the second section, mondo grass surrounds a small orange tree (both need water; the mondo grass likes the shade under the orange tree). In the third are aloes and agaves with grasses (almost no water required). And in the fourth section are purple flaxes and silver-leafed plants; and some lilies that have long, grasslike leaves similar to the flaxes, and white and purple flowers (all like moderate quantities of water and sunlight; if the purple flax gets too little sun it will turn green).

I will admit not all of this was planned—we planted the orange tree when we moved in twenty-five years ago, and the lilies propagated themselves by sending out runners from a couple of plants a gardener friend gave me several years later. In addition there are other invaders—or rather, they were there before I laid out the garden—that I like and don't want to lose, like a crawling ground cover with deep green leaves and little purple flowers. I took some from dear Mr. Hawkins's yard after he died. He left his house to his nephew, and it was empty for a year before the nephew sold it. No one looked after the garden, so after a while I started watering, and one thing led to another. I have some lovely potted cactus that I'm sure Mr. Hawkins would have loved for me to have; and anyway the guy who lives there now has a back-breaking TV job

---

REMEMBER THE CLASS PHOTO RULE

It's a good idea to position plants that will eventually be tall behind their shorter friends—that way no one blocks the view. Of course, if you plant big clumps of the same plant together, this "rule" doesn't pertain. Or if you can ascertain that, for instance, five different kinds of yellow flower all have similar environmental needs, you could consider that a clump and vary the placement of tall and short specimens—the unifying color scheme will become the important factor. Or your theme could be a really way-out mixture of magenta and orange, whatever.

and as far as I can tell is never home, or at least never home and awake.

When planning your garden, remember that plants that flower and/or fruit require a good deal of care. Think about getting color from foliage—there are wonderful silver, purple, wine, brown, blue, creamy-white, even black-leafed plants. And they can be spotted or striped, or, for instance, silver on top and green underneath, which provides a nice effect when the wind blows. And, of course, there are all shades of green, from the palest of pale, to chartreuse, to the dark, dark green of railroad sleeper cars in Europe.

> **ASPECTS OF AGAVE**
>
> Agaves can look like spider webs, cabbages, or artichokes. When the conquistadors arrived in Mexico, the indigenous people used agaves for soap, food, rope, shoes, and pulque, which is sort of like beer.

Striped agave by the highway.

A new neighbor actually set up and executed the most potentially dangerous action I've heard of yet. There's a large stand of blue agave in a kind of no-man's-land nearby. No one who lives across the small lane from the plot seems to take care of it—it's even full of poison oak. My neighbor hired a couple of men to dig up the plants, supplying them with those orange street maintenance vests and traffic cones, so they looked official. They also cleaned up some of the brush there to make the whole thing seem on the up and up. They did real well for a couple of hours, then someone called the police. Frustrated, because the guys were instructed to speak no known language, the cops finally just chased them off. And now my neighbor has a wonderful desert landscape of at least fifty blue agaves, which makes me green with envy.

Then consider fragrance—if you manage to capture and rear a lemon-scented eucalyptus, plant it next to the path leading to your house—so every time you step on fallen leaves you'll get a lovely whiff. Put two lilac bushes on either side of your front door; rosemary to brush against, creeping herbs like lemon thyme between stepping stones—you get the idea.

Keep spiny and spiky plants *away* from human contact. Don't plant them near footpaths or next to your door. It's no fun stepping barefoot on a dead holly leaf, or getting your new cashmere caught on a huge cactus spine. Unless, of course, you'd like to keep out unwelcome human (and even animal) intruders. For that purpose, plant a Natal plum under your bedroom window and listen to the howls as Mr. Bogeyman is pierced by thick, inch-long spines. The flowers have a gorgeous scent, and the fruit is delicious and strange and definitely edible—I skidded on a ripe, fallen one, three days prior to my writing this sentence.

And, one final thing: the noise factor. You're not going to find too much in the way of sound-producing flora, but I'm thinking about the huge, wonderful old cottonwood trees bordering a river where we stayed at a New Mexico bed and breakfast years ago—the rustle of their leaves in the breeze. (As in "... listen to the murmur of the cottonwood trees / Send me off forever but I ask you please / Don't fence me in.") The sound put me into a dream state. The wind screaming through tall pine trees is dramatic—when I'm not worrying if they're going to topple over onto the house. I don't suppose there are any sound-producing plants that don't need wind, except for Mexican jumping beans, which also move. So, if you want sound, give some thought to the wind patterns around your abode. The breezes you get are also useful to note regarding scent. (One nice aspect of living in a wet climate is that the rain will bring out the scent of your plants.)

Adapted weed patch. Notice how garden is divided into several distinct areas.

BETWEEN THE BARRACKS

Even if you have a tiny plot (like my front garden, which is twenty by ten feet), paths can make a garden mysterious, organized, intriguing, fun—whatever. Paths are not only an easy way to enhance the magic of your garden, they are also a necessity—they enable you to get close to your plants so you can tend to them. As with my little front garden, they can serve to divide different kinds of plants or plants with different needs. Paths also make little gardens seem much bigger—if you line them with tall plants, you won't know what's ahead when you turn the corner. If you have a beautiful view, you can hide it until the path leads you straight to it. If you have a long, narrow plot, you can make your path wander, open up at a central point (maybe a little pond, or a café table and chairs), and continue on its way.

Paths can be formal and direct, like those in an eighteenth century French herb garden, or meandering and leading to secret nooks. They can create separate "rooms."

You can pave a path with gravel, bark chips, natural stone from around where you live, bricks, or broken cement set in the earth to ground level. Whatever material you use, be sure that water can seep through it so you don't have standing puddles or slick spots—potential grounds for litigation. A tiny ground cover (preferably scented), growing in the earth between pieces, makes a paved path all the more attractive. You can leave the natural earth as I do, or if you have a meadow garden, mow yourself a path through the grasses and wildflowers.

If your path has to be narrow, edge it with plants like lavender so that when you brush against them you get a waft of scent. I hide things

---

ANTI-PERSONNEL PLANTS

When you go out on a foraging mission for cactus and other succulents, be sure to wear heavy (preferably leather) gloves. Bring a big rag, which you can fold and wrap around spiny varieties to steady them as you break off a cutting.

along my pathways because I don't have the room for a secret fountain or a garden seat—there's a little cement frog peaking out from some ground cover (Big Guy's name means "frog" in Italian). And barely visible, tucked in the thick grape ivy bordering one side, is a baby blue practice bomb—really—I guess it's from World War II. I bought it for my son when he was around ten. It was to be filled with sand and looks like a cartoon bomb, with fins on the bottom. There was one cement garden sculpture I lusted after—it was in an auction of property from a small museum—three little witches whispering to each other. I bid on it, but alas it sold for a lot of money. One of those things in life that you will always regret failing to pursue with a vengeance.

Remember my roommate Sue from college? Because Hurricane George was supposed to hit New Orleans, I called her to get the scoop. We had one of our yearly two-hour phone calls, during which time I made dinner and so on. She evacuated like everyone else, to a friend's house on higher ground, in Mississippi, where the hurricane actually did hit. Afterward, as they watched the city's wood chipper eating up downed trees, and because the ground was good and wet, they decided to pull out all the brush in the neglected next-door lot and put it on the curb for the guys with the chipper. And so a little beautification came out of an otherwise not very pretty event.

SPECIAL QUARTERS FOR SPECIAL CAPTIVES

You might enjoy growing one or more of the following, slightly unusual kinds of gardens. They're variously suited to tiny plots, various climates, your bathroom window ledge, pretty lazy gardeners, obsessive types, and so on.

cactus gardens

Meant to be planted willy-nilly, cactus gardens are for showing off all the different varieties you've captured. They're real easy to do indoors too, with miniature varieties, and you can even do a variation on an alpine garden (see following) with those same tiny cactus and succulents, plus palms, grasses, and bamboos. Just make sure you don't use granite, but collect stones, especially rounded ones, that look like they came from the desert, or actually did.

Cactus and other succulents are just about the easiest plants to propagate, because cuttings or plantlets carry their own supply of water with them so they don't risk dehydration if you forget to water twice a day (just kidding) in the crucial first days of planting. Your planting medium can be 100 percent coarse sand, which provides excellent drainage, a necessity for cactus and succulents. Without really good drainage, the planted part will rot and kill the whole thing. You can also get a bit lazy and plant them right

Agave in my neighbor's yard.

where they're going to stay, if you live in the right climate. (But you'd be surprised at how hardy some are—my sister in Oklahoma has a prickly pear growing out back, and it gets mighty cold in the winter where she lives.)

Even if you live in a wintry climate, you can still do a faux desert garden by planting stands of bamboo and ornamental grasses (see chapter 4) that are hardy in your area; intersperse them with potted cactus and succulents that you can bring inside for the winter. Ideally put them on your "sun porch"—we had one where I grew up in the New Jersey suburbs, with windows on three sides and no heat, yet I doubt that it ever got colder than fifty degrees in there.

Most cactus gardens are planted with plenty of space, left bare or sprinkled with gravel, between specimens. This is partly because each plant lusts after its full quota of sun, and partly because stalks, paddles, and the like tend to die off when they overlap. Some of my favorite large cactus include organ pipe cactus, prickly pear, Christmas cactus, agave, cereus, barrel cactus, and pencil cactus. To fill out the garden, you could sprinkle some low-growing plants among the big ones. Some of my choices for low-growing desert plants are: hen and chicks, hedgehog cactus, gasteria, pincushion cactus, and sea urchin cactus. They all produce offsets (baby plantlets still attached to the big plant) that are very easy to gather—some just drop off when you touch them.

alpine gardens

We used to call these rock gardens—where I grew up, every house had one out front. Now they're called "alpine," and to tell the truth they're much more interesting and varied now. They're meant to display the tiny plants that manage to sprout in the cracks of the granite of high mountains during a brief summer. If you live in the right climate (like the northeast or northwest) you can create a classic alpine garden; but they're no problem in any climate, and are especially useful if you have a very small plot to fool around with. You can try the same idea with rocks and plants native to your area that stay low to the ground and don't spread too much (although you can keep cutting them back, but that's work).

What you need to do first is to build your garden with rocks—some really big ones too, if you can borrow a real strong back and a truck. You'll want to approximate a mountainous slope, burying the rocks halfway and leaving space between them where your tiny specimens can put down roots.

Just as I wrote that last, I flashed on a roadside scene in Switzerland 1954—we were doing the Grand Tour in a huge Citroen Familiale (a seven-passenger sedan that my father bought for the trip and sold when we went home). We stopped to look at the tiny, yes, alpine flowers, my sisters and I climbing up the slope in our "good" clothes, which is how you traveled back then. Anyway, alpine flowers really exist in nature, I am here to say.

Once you have your rocks in place (or even make use of a natural rocky slope if you're lucky enough to have one), you have to add to/amend your soil. The best mix is one-third coarse sand, one-third compost, and one-third topsoil—very good drainage is a top priority. For mulch you can use coarse gravel, which will look like it belongs there.

By definition, alpine plants are tiny, and their offspring are so miniscule you need to use a magnifying glass if you're working with seeds. You'll definitely need tweezers and, if you really get into alpines, a scalpel. Be aware that all alpines need very good drainage, so babies should be started in pure coarse sand or a mixture of two-thirds sand and one-third peat moss.

If you are an obsessive type who liked, say, stamp collecting when you were young (like Big Guy), you can try growing alpines from seeds. You have to find them first—they can be hidden within the rosettes of cushion alpines (thus the magnifying glass)—they can take years to germinate in some cases, and everything, including the pot they're going in, should be sterile. Not for me.

It's much easier to propagate via cuttings and division (see chapter 3 for details) and you can use these methods on almost all types of alpine plants. Be warned, however, some stem cuttings will be only one-eighth-inch long. Take young shoots from the non-flowering stem tips all over the plant. Depending on the size of the mature plant, these will be up to four inches long. Trim to just below a leaf node and take off the leaves that otherwise would get buried. Dip cuttings in fungicide and rooting hormone and plant in pots or aluminum frozen-food trays, carefully water down the planting medium, then put the whole thing in a plastic bag in a coolish, lightly shaded place. You'll know that you've got roots when you get new shoot growth, and then you can put the plantlets in their own pots until they're hardier and ready to go into the garden.

Baby pine awaiting rescue.

You can try million bells, a tiny petunia-like flower; saxifrage, a real favorite—miniscule cushiony plants with tiny foliage and a profusion of flowers; gentian, which is a deep, deep blue; primroses; bellflowers; or mugo. Swiss mountain and dwarf white pines, Irish and Scotch mosses, creeping thyme, creeping baby's breath, and all sorts of miniature grasses and succulents are also good choices. You can plant leaves from sedum, a succulent much used in alpine gardens. Cut off the stem to the base of the leaf, and plant to one-quarter of its length. Don't water it too much or it will rot. More difficult is taking stem cuttings from cushion or carpet alpines. Their leaves are tiny rosettes, and you have to exercise care when you're taking them, which should be from the edges of the plant. Take as much stem as you can—it won't be more than one-half inch anyway. This is where you'll need tweezers, to hold onto the rosette while you cut it free and trim off the bottom leaves.

Fortunately there are alpines that send out self-rooting babies, which you can cut free and replant after you've trimmed off torn roots. Primrose is a prime example.

You can take root cuttings by lifting a whole plant and cutting off some thick roots near the crown. Then cut them into one-and-one-half-inch lengths, making a slanting cut at the bottom so that you'll know which end is up, and plant so that the tops are just under the rooting medium.

Finally, you can divide some alpines such as pinks and gentians, best done in early spring so you can put them right back into the ground next to the parent plant.

native plant gardens

A native plant garden, depending on where you try to grow it, may be reviled or even illegal. Ridiculous, isn't it? On the other hand, it may be welcomed as a way of protecting native habitat. Essentially it's made of wild plants gathered from right around where you live. For the purposes of making a wild garden, there are two kinds of plants you can gather, and one kind you shouldn't touch without expert help.

First, if you really want to help plants that are native to your area to thrive, the best way to go is to be sure that what you're gathering is native and not exotic—that is, introduced from other places. Practically every state has a native plant society (and a Web site), which will provide information about native and endangered plants.

Second, some wild plant life is so pervasive you might think it's native, only to find out that it's a marauder. If you just want a wild garden and don't care if it's native or not, take what you see a lot of (of course, it should be pretty or interesting), because then you won't be pulling out endangered plants.

Third, if you would really like to do some good, you can get more deeply involved, go through the proper channels, and eventually start raising endangered native plants.

My art dealer friend has what he calls his memory garden. He cared for his brother as he died of AIDS, and his first boyfriend, a hairdresser, also died of AIDS. He recalls a day when the boyfriend was trimming his brother's hair, and he looked past them through the window at the huge plants that had come from cuttings they gave him over the years. And now he looks at his memory garden every day as he sits at his kitchen table having his morning coffee.

Different parts of the country have different sorts of wild flora, of course, so your wild garden might be a prairie meadow, a desert habitat, a swamp meadow, a tropical jungle, or a quaint wildflower garden. There's a tremendous variety of attractive wild plants to choose from, including Queen Anne's lace, wild violets, black-eyed

Susans, buttercups, lady slippers, wood phlox, milkweed, wild asters, lupine, clover, maidenhair fern, wild onion, blazingstars, toyon, manzanita, deer grass, sages, monkey flower, rye, oats, buffalo grass, barley, ozark grass, foxtails, sedges—which are grasslike plants—cattails, and bulrushes. It's a pretty new concept, and there are actually soldiers out there saving this stuff from housing tract landscapers and agriculture. Many are flaunting laws against encouraging the growth of "weeds," if you can believe it.

Preparing the soil, even for wild plants, is important (it just means cultivating it to a depth of eighteen inches with no soil amendments). And you should plant lots of grasses that will spread and keep out unwanted plants. Otherwise, though, it's pretty simple. And capturing wild plants is usually perfectly safe, except where they have another kind of weed law (whereby you're not allowed to harvest native "weeds" in an area where endangered species exist). A wild garden, native or not, brings lots of birds, who will be foraging for all the bugs hiding within, and they and other animals will find places to live beneath the thick carpet of grasses and flowers that proliferate—without fertilizer or pesticides, very important—in their natural environment. You can start from seeds, which will take quite a while to flower, or uprooted plants (but it would do well to learn about endangered wild plants in your area before starting). Help the plants in your wild garden get established by watering at first.

One of my favorite native plant collections is a prairie garden. Prairie gardens grow where there are prairies, of course—Wisconsin, Kansas, the Dakotas, Oklahoma, Texas—the Great Plains—the big mid-section of the country. You have to mow paths through a prairie garden, and every couple of years you have to mow it down completely so that it can regenerate (mowing also exposes the earth to the sun). This is to duplicate how prairies evolved in the first place—via regular fires, set by Native Americans or started by lightning, which kept out trees, put nutrients back into the soil, and stimulated the growth of prairie grasses and flowers. If you live where you're allowed to do it, controlled burns are even better. A dry landscape is pretty easy to grow in some areas of the southwest, but you have to be aware of possible frosts, and you might not have much luck trying plants that grow on dry hillsides in your flat garden, which will probably retain moisture. You will have to water the first, establishing year.

ORNAMENTAL GRASSES

If you do a prairie or meadow garden, grasses will be the mainstay of your design. There are so many great-looking grasses, and because grasses are clumpers, you propagate them all the same way; by division, or by taking rooted plantlets or rhizomes with buds if the circumstances demand that you be less drastic.

> **BEES NEED WEEDS**
>
> Germany, which has no weeds (it's all that order and cleanliness), has 25 percent fewer honeybees than other northern European countries!

A favorite of mine, which most people consider a weed and which grows along the road, is pennisetum fountain grass. It makes lush green clumps up to thirty inches in diameter and has feathery, coppery-purplish flower spikes that don't really look like flowers. They grow without any water at all, even in gravel, die back in winter, and reappear in spring. You can't ask for much more than that.

Another grass that is useful for its color is gold hakone grass—some gardeners think it harmonizes with green better than white does. Dark green mondo grass does well in the shade and is very hardy—it seems that the blades never die. And there's pampas grass, which gets huge, with graceful big seed feathers—some planted themselves next to my pool years ago. Where they came from, I have no idea because no one else in the neighborhood has them. (You know by the very nature of this book that I snoop

Random roadside ornamental grass.

around in backyards.) There are sedges, which aren't true grasses but sure look like it—one of them turns a lush bronze color. There are tiny fescues, which you can plant in that alpine garden or cactus garden. Fescues have rolled leaves, like pine needles, not flat ones like most grasses. I once tried to seed my entire front yard with red fescue—they grow to about fourteen inches—so I could have a "lawn" without having to mow it, but alas I don't have enough sun, or I didn't use enough topsoil or something, and nothing happened.

To get some grass from a plant just cut through it, taking about one-quarter to one-third of the mother plant. I've found that fountain grass, for instance, needs strong biceps, so be prepared with a knife, saw, and sharp shovel, just in case. You can also give the plant a little tug, however, and if it gives a bit that means it's easy to harvest. Use two garden forks back-to-back to separate your clump from the mother plant. Put some fungicide on torn roots, as usual. Cut the grass back to six to eight inches before replanting. You can use a soil-based potting mixture and put your clump or clumplets in pots until they're full of new roots, then put them in the ground.

Of course, you can grow grass from seed. Cut off the "flower"—called the inflorescence—once it's fully mature and open. Let it dry for a few days, and then strip off the seeds or shake it over a large piece of paper. Gather the seeds, prepare your seedbed with soil-less seed mix, and plant, but not too close together. Cover with a shallow layer of soil.

water gardens

Then, of course, there's water.

If you have a natural source of water, consider yourself blessed. You can dam up a brook and have both the sound of running water and a pond where you can grow water plants—and watercress and mint along the banks of the brook. If, like most of us, the only source of water in your yard is the hose, you can actually make little waterfalls over a pile of rocks. (These can be real or fake, and you can carve them with little pockets to enhance the cascading and splashing effect.) The water falls into a pond and then recirculates back up via a pump. You'll need to buy the pump and build the pond (just dig a hole and cement it, or line it with rubber), which you can find in water gardening catalogs. You can raise goldfish or mosquito fish (to eat mosquito larvae) in the pond, because the falling water will provide oxygen, and you'll also want to put in water lilies, water hyacinth, water poppies, water snowflakes, papyrus, and the like to make more oxygen. You'll also attract birds who will come for a drink or a bath, and hopefully not raccoons and cats who will like the goldfish sushi.

You can also do all of the above on a much more modest scale, and even indoors with artificial light. You'll need a strong pot—really heavy-duty plastic is best in this case—they make great ones

Living in Ireland years ago and hearing interminably about cress sandwiches, I finally had one in a tearoom. Cress is not the same as watercress—the leaves are tiny, and it has none of the bite that makes our version so delicious.

now from recycled materials, which is in philosophical alignment with this manual. But I've also been eyeing the galvanized metal feed troughs at the barn where I buy my dogs' food in bulk. You won't need a pump, just some water plants to keep the water clean, a couple of snails for the algae, and some topping off when the water level goes down. As long as you have plants in your little water garden, you can keep goldfish in it, which will grow to a happy old age there.

For a simpler outdoor fountain you can use a large jardiniere, with the water flowing over the sides into a catch basin and back

A very small jardiniere with goldfish.

When we were thinking of moving once, we found a great house, but Big Guy said he knew he would go crazy listening to the Porsches changing gears on the winding canyon road below (movie agents going home to the Valley). So I actually hired a sound engineer to record the traffic at rush hour and lay the sound of a fountain over it. It worked, but then Big Guy said we wouldn't be able to hear the birds and so on. Not exactly true, but we didn't buy it, and just as well because it was totaled in the 1994 earthquake, and we never would have had earthquake insurance (we sure do now). If you live where noise is bothersome, a water garden with a fountain might help.

up again via the pump. A neighbor has a unique 1950s fountain of three bowls. The water cascades from one to another and then—it seems—into the ground, which is an area of large white rocks. Obviously, there's a receptacle down there, which catches the water and sends it back up to the top bowl via the supporting legs of the bowls. She has a very handy boyfriend who installed it (I watched—it wasn't easy), which is a useful piece of equipment to have in your garden wars.

Or if the windowsill scenario appeals to you, you can buy one of those baby fountains that I've begun seeing in doctors' waiting rooms—I guess to calm you down while you wait a couple of hours past your appointment time. A portable fountain probably won't mask the sound of huge trucks going over that pothole in front of your apartment, but it's worth a try. You can even make a (soundless) baby water garden in a pot for your coffee table, filled with dwarf water plants like floating fern.

There's one water feature I've always wanted, but alas my land (my hill, I should say) doesn't allow for it. European aristocrats were doing it centuries ago—using primitive technology—and you can do it too if you have a flat pad with low-growing plants near a path. Lay PVC pipe under the earth, with hidden sprinkler heads, which activate via laser beam when someone walks by, giving them a short spritz—a water joke. Of course, your cat will probably divorce you and move next door.

POND FLOWERS

If you're lucky enough to locate a big pond full of water plants, it's a good idea to help the owner (if there is one) by pulling up plants around the perimeter and replanting in the center, where, without your help, they tend to die off like grasses. They can also grow out of control, upsetting the ecology of the pond, in which case they have to be cut back drastically. So while you're at it, you can take some for yourself. Water plants grow either free-floating, like water hyacinth, or rooted in the mud below, like most water lilies, with much of their top-growth underwater too. So planting them out requires methods different from all others.

Almost all water garden plants can be propagated by division. This is also the easiest way to start off new plants, because all you have to do is mimic their normal growing conditions. Cuttings and seeds are much more particular.

Cut off a hunk of roots and leaves, and wash very carefully to remove algae from the entire plant. If you must save the parent plant, you can just lift it out of the water without tearing it loose and put it back when you've done your surgery. If you've got small divisions, plant them in heavy soil or a soil-based potting mix in small pots, which you will then have to put into a big tub filled with water to the level of the soil. When the new plants are established, you'll want to put them into mesh baskets—if you're doing a baby water garden, you can use those green plastic baskets that strawberries are sold in. Water must be able to move freely through the roots of a water plant.

Some floating water plants make plantlets on long stems, which eventually rot and break off by themselves, causing the plantlet to float away if you don't get to it first. When you do, put it in the soil potting mix up to its crown, cover that with a bit of gravel, and submerge the plant in water as just described. Divide other floaters like water hyacinth and put them in water, supporting the babies upright until they find their footing by themselves, via air sacs at the base. They will soon be making new plantlets.

moonlight gardens

Whenever we walk up the stairs after the movies, from the garage to the house, we pass our Natal plum hedge, which has exotically scented flowers that somehow emit their fragrance more at night. Same with the orange tree, when it blooms twice a year—the scent is better at night. I breathe deep and am transported to somewhere like Morocco or Cairo for a second—scent, of course, is the most primitive sense in humans, and so the most evocative. A moon garden is based on this idea: heavily scented and/or white or cream flowers, so you can experience them in the dark. If you have the right climate, try the plants I just mentioned. Other good alternatives for an evening garden include white roses, angel's trumpets, callas, night-blooming jasmine, white honeysuckle, hyacinths, lilac, primrose, and tuberose, whose scent is intoxicating—my favorite. Or grow some silvery-gray or white-leaved plants. Find out what flowers are night-scented where you live and start borrowing cuttings. To make them all stand out, intersperse very dark green leafy plants and a real dark mulch. And keep it close to your house, because you're not going to go walking in the dark in the middle of the night to get to it. If you have a deck you can plant beneath it. You can even grow it on an apartment terrace.

Anyway, the point is to have some sort of plan—you can even do it in the month or two that your first babies are sprouting roots, before you have to put them in the ground. Be prepared, though, to make turn-on-a-dime tactical changes—this is war, after all.

My old boss told me that when his parents retired to the south of England, they used to tour grand houses and castles open to the public, mainly to gather cuttings.

SURVEILLANCE AND RECONNAISSANCE

It's always a good idea to get to know the territory before you make a true advance. Here are some tips on pinpointing areas of attack—from your own block to Tierra del Fuego or wherever.

As you drive or walk by areas where there is plant life, make it second nature to be on the lookout for possible prey. A couple of times, I've put a major strain on Big Guy's heart by screeching to a stop by a tiny treelet growing bravely next to the road.

INFILTRATION

Make friends of potential enemies:

- Gardeners
- Tree pruners
- Trash collectors
- Neighbors
- Real estate agents
- Hikers
- Public maintenance crews
- Doormen
- Security guards
- Busybodies

---

your neighborhood

Examine the edges of private property for untended forgotten plants. You can identify them by looking for surrounding weeds, the absence of sprinklers, an unpruned look to your target, or dead growth still attached to the plant.

strolling around the town

Identification is similar to that of checking out your neighborhood; however, you need to be surreptitious because you are in less familiar territory, and people might be spying from behind curtains. You might just mistake a cherished pet for a weed. It's better to make a few forays before actually attacking.

An acquaintance mentioned a beautiful stand of cannas in front of a tall office building (which I had actually noticed myself and had mentioned to a friend just that morning). I love the weird color combination of scarlet (the flowers) and wine (the leaves). Anyway, she asked me how she could acquire some of these wonderful flowers—should she go at night? I told her, "Uh-uh, you're not getting it; that would be rather illegal. What you have to do is find the building's operations manager, tell him you own a commercial building that needs landscaping and you love what his people do, and could you have their name and number? Then call them and ask what their schedule is so you can come watch what they do when they change out the cannas. Then you can ask for them, and you'll probably get the whole bed, not just a scraggly plant or two." I never said it wasn't work.

parks

Public parks are always a tempting challenge, and it's best to go when the park is at its emptiest. Of course, you must take care to avoid ambush by guards or much more undesirable types who will certainly outgun you, with your spade and clippers.

open country

It's arguably no-holds-barred in this terrain with one important caveat: do some research first regarding endangered flora. You really do want to leave that area alone—a good soldier plays by the rules.

roadside

Try to put your mobile unit between yourself and passing motorists for camouflage, protection from flying missiles, and a quick get-away as soon as you accomplish your mission. This tip applies whether the raid was spontaneous or planned ahead.

A very organized, corporate sort of guy I know, Rick, is a bonsai gardener. Within the culture, bonsai masters call their guerrilla gardening "gathering." Very polite. For the best potential bonsais, they go to some windswept cliff to find a gnarled, stunted old tree, probably really rare and special, and retrieve it—the whole thing. Then you stunt it some more, like Chinese foot-binding.

empty lots

Generally, an empty lot is considered fair game, unless it looks like construction is imminent—then be careful.

transition properties

Properties between active ownership, such as construction sites, long-vacant houses, and long-empty commercial buildings can provide some desirable loot. Of course, if the area is fenced off or No Trespassing signs are displayed, I would advise you to avoid the area. Where I live, restaurants open and close with the frequency of movie runs, and luckily the creation of a unique ambience has become a major feature of the dining experience. I often see expensive plants abandoned after each failed incarnation, there for the taking.

My bonsai friend regularly used to forage behind plant nurseries, where dying or otherwise undesirable plants are tossed. He found a wonderful, small, root-bound pine, and being honest brought it to the nurseryman, wanting to buy it. The owner said, "I can't sell it to you." He just wouldn't sell it. So finally Rick said, "Okay, will you give it to me?" "Yes," the owner said. It became a fabulous bonsai, which Rick sold for a fortune along with his other specimens when he moved across the country.

easements

An easement is a right of passage over a neighbor's land, and most easements are granted to private parties. Here, I'm referring to the little pockets or strips of land on which phone companies and other utilities place their equipment. There's one near my house that has particularly lush plant life that's crept over from the house next to it. I keep meaning to go on a raid, but every time I pass it I have my infant granddaughter with me, and my son would never speak to me again if the two of us got carted off to jail.

municipal and commercial properties

Keep an eye out for landscaped areas. When gardens are changed frequently to maintain freshness, there's bound to be some valuable discards. I've even seen little gas station gardens—surrounded by Astroturf—tended to regularly.

other potential sites

- Trash (residential and dumpsters)
- Behind nurseries (especially if the business is moving or closing down)
- Botanical sale throwaways
- Alleyways
- Anything that is growing over onto your property
- Sidewalk cracks
- Branches, nuts, and the like that have fallen off the parent plant
- Beaches (don't take grass strategically planted to shore up dunes)
- Private property when you ask permission
- Private property when it looks very unloved, and only sparingly, and around the perimeter
- Private property when it's absolutely huge, and only if it's untended (again, the area around the perimeter is probably the best spot—also advisable for a quick getaway)

WEAPONS AND GEAR

To free the masses huddled along roadsides, in abandoned parking lots, behind gas stations, drying up in front of closed-down banks and to bring democracy to the elitist pastime of gardening (i.e., it's cheap), you will need the following:

- A small spade
- A sharp knife
- Clippers
- Shovels—one ordinary, sharp spade-shaped; and a collapsible weapon for your mobile unit or while traveling on secret missions
- Loppers for thick branches
- A saw for really tough roots
- A tree pruner if you're really ambitious or lust after something you can't capture otherwise
- Two garden forks (like little rakes), for the plant division method of propagating
- Containers for gathering—cardboard boxes or plastic garbage bags are best; recycle used plastic market bags
- Containers for planting—egg cartons, small pots, or plastic bags to cover
- A mister—such as an empty Windex bottle, totally washed out
- Aluminum foil and wet paper towels—for fast-wilting plants/all-day forays
- Rooting hormone; also called root toner

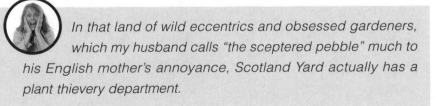

In that land of wild eccentrics and obsessed gardeners, which my husband calls "the sceptered pebble" much to his English mother's annoyance, Scotland Yard actually has a plant thievery department.

Be creative. Find out who cares for your local gas station garden.

- Fungicide (more on this and rooting hormone in the next chapter)
- Divets—anything than can make a hole in the earth for your cutting, pencil-sized or narrower—ideally various-size dowels
- Rubber boots
- Gardening gloves
- Thick clothing, in case you have to scramble under or over barbed wire or through brambles
- Disguises—sunglasses, a cap (under which you can hide long hair, if you have it)
- This field manual
- Area maps—if you're going far afield, on dirt roads, and the like. And if you're rich enough not to even need this manual, a global positioning device would be nice.

An employee of a top garden designer I know has an uncle in Wales who wears a great big overcoat. The inside of the coat is completely lined with little pockets in which to hide cuttings he gathers on his travels.

Finally, it's a good idea to wear long sleeves and long pants regardless of the time of year. You'll want protection against insects and poisonous plants.

The best guerrilla is one who is ready for all situations. If most of your forays are by mobile unit, keep an "emergency" kit at hand all the time: be prepared. I even leave a big old blanket in mine, for wrapping large or thorny specimens.

CHAPTER THREE

CAPTURE AND CARE
OF PRISONERS

Many plants flourish only in certain climates. Others grow in almost any part of the country. You're really safe only when you're waging war on your own turf. Of course, your first efforts at visual identification of your prey will be hit or miss. Obviously, it is helpful to be able to recognize what you're looking for, and with practice, you'll get better at it.

If you do spot some prey elsewhere, in a climate very different from your own, you'll have to accept the reality that your capture is likely to die if it gets even a whiff of your Minnesota frost, or will have to go through a cold, dormant period in the old fridge where you keep your beer if you live in Key West. Even with the best of care it might not ever be a happy soldier. Furthermore, some plants take to propagating much more easily than others.

Other plants, like mint and watercress, proliferate wildly, but they must be started from a rooted plant. Some, like baby tree seedlings, don't much like being moved and can't take a lot of sun or water—you have to be watchful, as with a newborn baby, and do it just right.

And if you are after a tree full of delicious fruit, you'd better look in a gardening encyclopedia to make sure your date tree can pollinate itself (with a little help from the birds and the bees) or whether you need a male and a female tree. There's no doubt that some research can come in quite handy. Is it worth it with this kind of gardening? You're not trying to be Luther Burbank, after all.

And finally, you don't want to capture an endangered plant or even its seeds. So if you have any doubts, leave it alone—there are plenty of other trees in the forest, as the saying goes.

Someone I met recently at a dinner party told me about her close friend, the late composer John Cage, who was a formidable mushroom hunter. She accompanied him on his searches a few times, which was when she found out that his favorite battlefields were the lawns in front of shopping malls and suburban houses. With the latter, he was always very proper, ringing the doorbell first and asking permission to harvest.

I've learned by making mistakes. I've watched stuff die after a particularly hazardous capture (in transit too long, too much or too little water, too much or too little sun, the wrong earth). Some plants would simply rather give up the ghost than live in captivity. You'll make mistakes too, but don't give up the good fight.

Under ideal circumstances, your guerrilla gathering should be done with the best interests of the plant in mind. If you can't provide a plant with what it likes and needs, at least give it conditions that it can tolerate. And don't be greedy. Pass up war-ravaged patches so they can heal themselves first, unless after longtime surveillance you conclude that intervention is the only option. When you do plunder, do it with a light hand so that it won't really be noticeable to the plant or the landscape. If you see other guerrillas in a zone, back off and find another battle to wage somewhere else.

And remember: when you are in attack mode, be alert, use those eyes behind your head, and work under cover of darkness unless circumstances indicate that this is more dangerous than operating in plain sight, which is a skill well worth learning. (A foray into New York's Central Park, for instance, should not be conducted in the wee hours.) As to operating in plain sight, I've seen movie stars doing it—no makeup, pimples, thick glasses, dirty hair, and clothes you wouldn't go to the market in. No one recognizes them, excepting old eagle eye, a star worshipper from way back. On the other hand, though, Alan Funt of *Candid Camera* once said, and I think it's true, "Half the people notice everything all the time, and half the people notice nothing ever." Anyway, look nonchalant, look like you belong there, and don't make eye contact unless you have to. I have found that this "invisible" camouflage, when perfected, nearly always works unless you are in someone's front yard.

PREPARING YOUR BARRACKS

Although it may not be particularly glamorous work, you'll want to be ready to care for your new plants as soon as you get them to their destination. So before I talk about how to take your prisoners, I'll first discuss preparing their nurseries.

rooting medium

You might decide to throw caution to the wind and just stick your cuttings in the ground, but you'll get better results if you use a rooting medium. This is an almost comically confused area. Every self-proclaimed expert will give you different advice. You'll be told to plant in peat moss, coarse peat moss (which will not break down, harden, and shed water like regular peat moss), perlite, vermiculite, sand, or very coarse sand (which unlike sand will allow water to drain through and air to stay in). Turkey grit, gravel, mulch, redwood bark, foam packing peanuts, sterile ground pumice, crushed lava, et cetera, will also be recommended. Some people hate vermiculite, which is an artificial product and therefore contains no bacteria; others love perlite, because it's a natural product, and natural is better. Some say use all sand so that water will drain right through, some give you complicated recipes for one-third this, one-sixth that, and so on.

The first thing to remember, if you want to do it right (I'm the first to admit I don't always follow my own advice) is this: don't use dirt from your garden because it could be diseased or become compacted, not allowing tiny roots to grow. If there was ever topsoil near your house it was undoubtedly scraped down to bare clay during construction.

Second, it would seem logical to use potting soil, but don't, because you're not planting actual plants yet, with intact, developed roots and a full leaf system.

Third, I would say that a mixture of equal parts of coarse sand and peat moss is the safest way to go if you get bored with the whole process. Use all coarse sand in the case of cactus and succulents, which as we all know don't like too much water. What you mainly need to remember is that your rooting medium should be light and airy.

Rooting hormone, also called root toner, is a very important tool that really does help your little prisoners thrive. It's available in powder and liquid form, which you have to dilute, the ratio depending on the sort of cutting you're treating. Rooting hormone stimulates root development, targeting only the tip of the cutting. Some root toners include fungicides, but even so, when immersing a number of cuttings, don't dip the cutting into the jar—this could cause diseases to spread. Pour a bit out into another container and dunk your cutting in this. Whatever you do, never return used rooting hormone to its original container. Throw it out. To keep a super clean environment, it's best to also buy fungicide and dip cuttings in that first to kill off germs—cuttings are like newborns, and even dirty hands can pose a threat.

containers

You can plant your seeds and cuttings in very small pots for singles, or larger pots for five or six seeds or plantlets (layering, root division, planting rhizomes, dropping—all discussed later in this chapter—take place right in the ground). For really tiny seeds and cuttings, you can use a disposable aluminum cake pan from the market, and plant in rows, or milk cartons cut lengthwise with some drainage holes in the bottom. Styrofoam take-out cups, boxes, and freezer-to-microwave one-dish meal containers also work. Make some drainage holes in all of these too. Best of all are the little black plastic pots from the nursery, the kind that get tossed out. Plastic retains moisture much better than terra cotta, which is a big plus when doing this delicate business.

> **GIVE YOUR BABY PLANTS A BREAK**
>
> How do you know that your roots are taking? Don't stick your dirty finger in (really—serious gardeners keep everything around baby plants hospital-clean, dipping all tools in a tablespoon of bleach mixed with a quart of water) and don't tug, roots at this stage are tiny and fragile and this can tear them. You have to trust the condition of the stem. Is it healthy-looking? Also note if the original leaves of the cutting are thriving. If everything aboveground looks okay, then you can assume that everything below is okay too.

Mini-greenhouses have the added advantage of maintaining the humid atmosphere infant plants need, and they're easy to make. For cuttings and leaf cuttings, fill a twelve-inch pot with rooting medium. Then plug the drain hole of a four-inch unglazed terra cotta pot with silicone sealer and nest the small pot in the

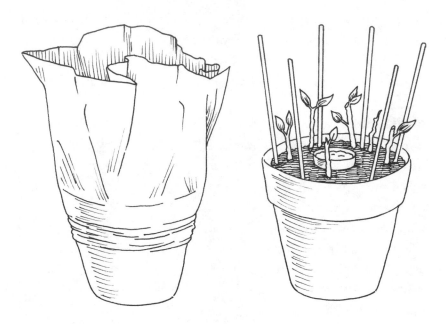

A mini greenhouse.

center of the soil in the large pot. Insert cuttings in a circle around the large pot, two or three inches apart, then put six sticks or skewers, each about twelve inches high, between the cuttings. Water the cuttings lightly, then fill the small pot with water. Place the whole thing in a large transparent plastic trash bag and close with a twist tie at the top (the skewers will support the bag). Put in dappled sunlight. As the water in the small pot evaporates, you will have a self-humidifying greenhouse. Check the water level in that pot every other day, and when your cuttings have rooted you can plant them and start the process over again (you can be more ambitious and make five or six baby greenhouses, too).

My son used to raise snakes, and I inherited one of his large terrariums when his new wife put her foot down—actually I saved it from the trash when they moved. It came in real handy when I rescued a baby squirrel and raised him to adolescence— I loved that squirrel. And now I raise other babies in it, green ones (seeds, cuttings, and leaf cuttings). It has a screen top, which I cover with plastic in the critical initial stages when the cuttings need humidity.

If you're going to plant your cuttings directly into the ground, you can make private greenhouses for all of them. Collect large plastic soft drink or water bottles, and with a sawtooth-edged knife, cut off the bottom one-and-one-half inches (or you can use a knife heated over a gas flame). Keep the screw-on top. Put the bottle, right side up of course, over the cutting. You'll see that the moisture that collects on the sides of the bottle will drip back down into the soil around the plant. If it's hot you can take off the cap, or if it's really hot you can prop up a side with a stone. If it's real windy, you can put a stick through the bottle's neck and drive it into the ground so it won't blow away. You can also make individual bottle greenhouses to go into terra cotta pots that are slightly larger in diameter.

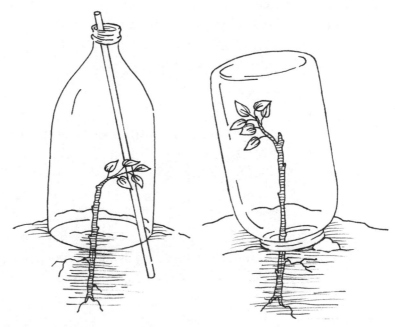

Private "greenhouses" for in-the-ground cuttings.

SEEDS

If you feel bad about uprooting a whole tree (or more likely, aren't strong enough to do it), you can gather its seeds. Or you can plant seeds of fruit and vegetables from your kitchen, but I usually toss this stuff down the hill, for the birds, squirrels, and mice, because commercially grown food usually comes from hybrids and won't emerge true to type. The progeny are most often inferior to the parent anyway. A hybrid is a kind of mongrel, a combination of two or more species, that is created by agriculturalists and rabid gardeners by grafting. (Grafting actually first occurred naturally between wild grasses rubbing together, which produced wheat— the beginning of agriculture!) Anyhow, you'd do better to pick up the fallen fruit of a noncommercially grown plant or tree.

Some seeds root more easily than others. Broadly, seeds from annuals (plants that live for one year) root the most easily; then perennials (plants that survive year to year, even if they go dormant in winter); and lastly biennials (which live for two years). Note that if you want to harvest seeds from your biennial, you might have to protect it during the winter. Biennials don't make seeds until their second year.

My doctor's mother and her best friend, Bernie, lived in a small town in Utah. Bernie had a really wonderful garden, and she used to give Dr. B's mother cuttings from it all the time. Bernie lived at the edge of a stream, however, and one day it became a raging torrent, wiping out the garden she cherished more than anything else. You know what's coming: Dr. B's mother promptly returned the favor, and Bernie's garden grew again. And then, years later, Bernie went into a retirement community; and, of course, she brought bushels of cuttings with her, like an artist who would not think of leaving his paints and brushes when he moves.

Barbara and her unidentified tropical fruit trees.

I have a virtual little forest of live oaks on my hillside, born of fallen seeds from three mature trees. Even seedlings around a foot high have very long taproots and are hard to transplant, though, so if I want to move them around I have to keep my eyes open for real babies, which hide among the other plant life there. And someone recently told me that you can't legally cut down any live oak with a trunk diameter of more than one inch—which, in ignorance, I have done. Somehow, though, this smells like the urban myth about tearing off the labels on pillows and mattresses—who's going to arrest you?

I recently potted an ash seedling from a neighbor's yard, and it's grown nicely over the summer in partial sun—it actually looks like a little tree already, with a hardwood trunk. A few years ago, I potted the large seeds of a tropical fruit tree from the garden of an artist I know. I'd tasted some of the fallen fruit, and it was fabulous.

But no one recognizes either the little trees or my description of the fruit, which tastes like custard. I've got three trees, hoping that if they're not self-pollinating (see following) I've at least got a male and a female. (Maybe you know what they are; the fruit is green and the size and shape of a smallish apple, but the tree is not a custard apple.)

Seeds from fruit won't always produce fruit. Some plants are monoecious—that is, both male and female flowers occur on a particular plant. Others are dioecious—meaning that a particular plant will have only male flowers or female flowers. As I mentioned earlier, both types require pollen bees, or wind, or you, like a sex therapist, to do the pollinating—transferring the pollen from a male flower to a female flower, which it then fertilizes. This is called cross-pollination. Asparagus, date palms, hazelnut, kiwi, papaya, Smyrna figs, and spinach are all dioecious plants.

The only plants you won't have trouble with are those that are self-pollinating, that is, they need no assistance to pollinate, because each flower is bisexual and they do it all themselves. Although they're more likely to bear healthy fruit if the pollen goes from one flower to another, I'd definitely stick with these for starters.

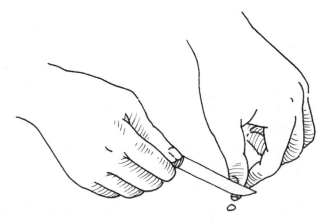

Cutting away some hard seed coating.

You have to wait until seeds are ripe (in most cases, when they've fallen to the ground), and before they are rotten, to plant.

seeds with hard shells

The shells are there for a reason—they protect the seed against hostile conditions like cold or drought until it's time for it to germinate, and they actually contain a growth-stopping hormone. (In fact, some seeds germinate by contact with the chemicals released by smoke, a startling evolutionary adaptation meant to reseed forests after fires.) You can start the process by injuring the seedcoat by sandpapering, or squashing a bunch of them under the blade of a big knife, or soaking them overnight and then gently chipping away a bit. Whatever you do, don't injure the seed itself. And once you've done all this, you've got to plant the seed right away.

planting seeds

Most seeds should be planted in the spring. To keep seeds fresh, they have to be kept absolutely dry and cool. And don't keep them for too long. You're safest if you use them within a year, even though many seeds will germinate after years have passed—like those in the stomachs of Egyptian mummies. If you collect seeds in the fall for plants that grow naturally in cold climates, you'll have to over-winter them. To do so, put them in pots with damp peat moss and place them in a dark spot with a low temperature (35 to 45 degrees) for one to three months. If you live in a warm climate, put them in the fridge. Remember to keep moist. As a rule, these plants can't be grown indoors except when you're starting them.

One of the most common reasons why seeds fail is because they've been planted too deeply. Seeds have just enough energy in them to make roots and send up a tiny seedling, which, if it has too far to go, won't make it. The golden rule: depth should not exceed twice the diameter of the seed, which in most cases means it will barely be covered by soil.

Another cause of failure is overwatering. Like mature plants, only much more sensitive, seeds need a supply of moisture and air in the soil, and saturated soil drives out the air. The best planting medium for seeds is 70 percent peat moss and 30 percent coarse sand, which will provide good drainage. Fine sand won't—don't use it. Someone I know uses crushed lava with peat moss for palm seeds. Water very carefully after planting and let the seedbed almost dry out before watering again. Be sure to monitor the soil's dampness frequently—although overwatering is a problem, once seeds are planted, lack of moisture will cause them to dry out and die.

The third cause of seed death is temperature—too low or too high or too erratic. Unless you're going to become a professional, I would just wing it; you know a palm seed is going to need more heat than a maple seed. If you live where there can be freezing temperatures, wait until they're over to plant seeds. If your seeds are planted outside, you can cover them with plastic, which helps stabilize temperature and retain moisture.

Some seeds have a long period of dormancy, and you might plant them, do everything right, and still not get a plant. If you know your seeds aren't from annuals, which means they have to sprout, try planting some in a sheltered area of your garden and others in pots. They should sprout in one site or the other.

Wherever you live, you'll see plants that are much desired and sold in nurseries in their non-native climates, but grow wild in your own. Native plants are your best bet for propagating from seeds—that's what they're doing without anyone's help. They can be magnificent pines, wildflowers, grasses, rhododendrons, mountain laurel, cactus, and succulents, whatever—after all, everything that grows started out wild.

An alternate way to start some seeds is the way it's done with ferns. Collect the spores (which are similar to but different from seeds) from inside the blips underneath fern leaves. You'll have to shake out the spores when they're ripe (dark green but not brown and dead), which are miniscule. They need a fine film of moisture, so scatter them on blotting paper or a few layers of paper towel, which has to be kept moist at all times. Put the paper in a flat dish; cover it with something transparent, like the square top from a supermarket cake or a Pyrex dish; and place it in the shade. Eventually a green jelly will appear, and the plantlets will grow in it. At this point lift the entire piece of paper and lay it down on top of a container of peat moss, and water well. Cover it again with something transparent until the plants are on their own. The process can take a few months, so be patient. You can also try starting bromeliads, begonias, and rubber plants on wet paper.

STEM CUTTINGS

Cuttings from stems will be your typical capture. They're easy prey—just a quick, surreptitious snap or cut, and in my experience, they're the best survivors in captivity. General instructions: first, cut the stem one inch below a node or bud (where a new leaf is starting to appear). Then, at home, trim the stem to just below the node with a very clean knife (if you have a long enough stem, you can get a number of cuttings from one stem). Finally, snip off any flowers (but it's really better to take cuttings without flowers—all of the plant's energy will go to a flower or bud and not to the roots, where you need it) and leave only a few leaves. If the leaves are real big, cut them in half, again so growing energy will go into the roots. Each cutting should have at least two leaf nodes or buds, from which leaves grow.

And if everyone tells you what you're doing won't work, try it anyway—you never know.

There are three different kinds of stem cuttings, but they're all variations on a theme, depending on when in the growing season they're harvested—early spring, mid-summer, or just as the plant is going dormant. They must always be taken from the current year's growth, though—no old wood. They also differ in overall hardiness (the youngest are the least, the oldest, the most), and in the time they take to root (the youngest in a couple of weeks, the oldest in two to six months).

Stem cutting.

MANAGING EMERGENCIES

If you're not on a gathering mission but happen to spot a plant you must have a piece of, it's okay to break off a cutting, but when you get back to base make a clean cut with a very clean knife where the stem is torn before planting it.

What you don't want to do is to try to take cuttings from suckers unless I tell you to (as with succulents) in the pages that follow. These are strong sprouts that grow from the roots of a plant. In flowers that have been grafted, like roses, suckers will be growing from the rootstock, and they'll give you a different rose from the flowers on the plant. Suckers also tend to get diseases easily.

softwood cuttings

Cut softwoods in the spring, just as new growth—which is what you'll be taking—begins to harden (i.e., the stems will still be soft and pliable). Don't take them the week they appear on the mother plant because they'll most likely be too premature to survive on their own. It's preferable to take only tip cuttings—one cutting from each branch, which is the new growth. Strip the leaves off the bottom, leaving just the stem and a few leaves at the top. Wounding a cutting helps make roots—with a delicate softwood cutting all you have to do is to lightly scrape the cutting from the bottom up one-half inch. Dip in fungicide and rooting hormone.

Because softwood stems are not very rigid and will break if you push the stem itself into the planting medium, first make a hole with

> **SOFTWOOD SUCCESSES**
>
> Try the following plants for softwood cuttings:
> - Azalea
> - Birch
> - Camellia
> - Dogwood
> - English ivy
> - Forsythia
> - Gingko
> - Hibiscus
> - Hydrangea
> - Honeysuckle
> - Lavender
> - Lilac
> - Mint
> - Morning glory
> - Olive
> - Oregano
> - Rose
> - Rosemary
> - Sage
> - Tarragon
> - Thyme

a divet (or anything else you can make a hole with—a skewer, a disposable chopstick, a dowel—but be sure it's clean). You can also slice the medium with a trowel or putty knife. Don't let the earth get compacted around the hole, which will make it hard for tiny roots to power their way through. When dropping the cutting in, make sure that it makes good contact with the soil.

These babies need warmth, humidity, and shade. If they dry out, even for a couple of hours, you've lost them. So it's best to keep them under plastic bottles if you're planting directly into the ground, or put your pots into plastic bags closed with twist ties and water lightly and often in the first few days—until they root, which should be in a couple of weeks. Softwood cuttings are the best choice for indoor plants, in which case, put the pots in a north-facing window. When you capture softwood, don't soak the cuttings in water—this prevents the cut surfaces from healing, a process that needs oxygen. But don't let them dry out, either. Just wrap in a moist paper towel and put them in a baggie until you plant.

greenwood or semi-hard cuttings

Cut greenwood in summer, from the current year's growth, when the plant is still growing. Look for stems that are still green and soft at the tip but starting to harden at the base. You'll tend to find them at the top of a main shoot. Plant greenwood cuttings in loose soil and keep them moist, not wet. To reduce water loss, cut the leaves on the stem in half, especially if they're big. Greenwood cuttings take more time to root—three weeks to three months—than softwood cuttings, but stand a better chance of survival. Cut stems should be four to six inches long.

GREAT GREENWOOD CUTTINGS

Look for these plants for cuttings during the summer months:

- Bottlebrush
- Camellia
- Cedar
- Clematis
- Cypress
- Grapes
- Heather
- Hemlock
- Honeysuckle
- Holly
- Magnolia
- Mango
- Pine
- Pomegranate
- Privet
- Rhododendron
- Rose

hardwood cuttings

As with all types of cuttings, take the current season's healthy growth. The best time for taking hardwood cuttings is when the stems are fully mature, and even dormant—mid- to late autumn. The wood shouldn't bend. The cuttings should be four to twelve inches long and have two to four nodes or buds each. The top cut should be made just above a node and the bottom cut just below one.

You don't have to use only the new tips of branches as with soft-wood, but don't use late-season growth or weak branches. Some plants, like forsythia and grape, can grow many feet in one season, and you can get a whole bunch of cuttings from one branch. Just be sure that each one has two to four nodes. The bottom cut, just below a leaf node, will develop a callus to protect the wound, and the top cut, being above a node, will provide protection for the node, keeping the buds from being knocked off. Make a slant cut at the bottom and a straight cut at the top to make sure that you plant the cutting right side up. On deciduous plants or trees, remove all leaves. In temperate and warm climates, plant cuttings in shaded sun, sheltered from the wind.

> **HARDY HARDWOODS**
>
> Good sources for hard-wood cuttings include:
> - Black currant
> - Blueberry
> - Bougainvillea
> - Crape myrtle
> - Dogwood
> - Ficus
> - Fig
> - Holly
> - Mock orange
> - Mulberry
> - Poplar
> - Raspberry
> - Red currant
> - Sycamore
> - Willow

At a birthday barbecue, I sat with a European couple I had never met. I told them about this book: they told me about a friend of theirs, an immensely rich, self-made guy of forty who had sold his business and was bored to death. He bought a huge sea-front property in Saint-Tropez and wanted to plant lots of mature olive trees. Apparently you can't uproot mature olive trees in France. So he bought thousands of acres of olive groves in Andalusia and got his mature trees.

Bury one-half to two-thirds of the cutting. Once planted, hardwood cuttings should be watered when dry. They don't need heat while rooting.

Hardwood cuttings are more likely to survive than other cuttings, so it's worth waiting for them as they take their sweet time to root. Even if they put out new growth, they might not yet have roots. Roots will start at about three months—to see if they're started, you can pull very gently and see if you meet resistance. If you can wait, however, don't move the new plant for twelve months.

My famous garden designer friend regularly forages for mature trees in the gardens of older neighborhoods. Sometimes owners are happy to get $1,000, open to the sun what they suddenly realize is a too-shady backyard, and get a new landscape for free in the bargain. And she's gotten a great big palm or ficus for her client's otherwise naked little acre.

If you live in a climate where there are cold winters, you can take a lot of hardwood cuttings from a tree or plant that grows there naturally, tie them together, and label them in bunches of about ten. Store them upright so that the plant's products whose job it is to start the rooting process will go to the base of the cutting, where they're needed. Place them in a one-foot deep trench, filled with sand to cover, with the tops no more than one inch under the surface. This will form a callus, which is thick tissue that grows where the plant is injured, and which makes an ideal place for roots to start. Dig them up and plant in the spring.

An alternative method of winterizing hardwood cuttings is to cut and tie them together as just described, then cool them for two to four months at 50 to 55 degrees (your basement or garage). For the following two months, keep them at 35 to 40 degrees (in your fridge) to retard growth.

LEAF CUTTINGS

The capture of leaf cuttings is the easiest of all, and leaves behind an almost pristine mother plant, which is like practicing humane warfare, if there is such a thing. Once captured, however, this prisoner is more finicky than a stem cutting, I've found.

Take only thick, healthy, fleshy leaves. Look for leaves that are "adults"—neither too old nor too young. You can cut very large leaves in half, so energy will go to rooting. Plant upright, burying one-third of the leaf. Or you can make nicks at half-inch intervals in the main veins on the underside of the leaf (be sure to cut all the way through the vein) and lay the leaf flat on the

> **LUCK WITH LEAF CUTTINGS**
>
> Start new plants with the leaves of these:
> - African violet
> - Begonia
> - Cactus
> - Primrose
> - Sanseveria
> - Succulents

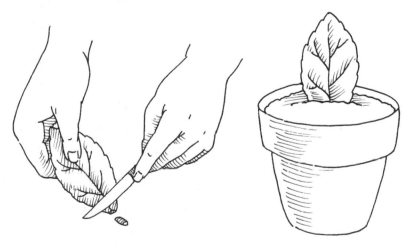

Planting a leaf cutting.

earth. Use pebbles to keep the cuts in contact with soil, water lightly, and cover with plastic to keep moist. New plants will root and grow from where you made the cuts. With very long succulent leaves, you can cut them into two-inch slices, dip in rooting hormone, and bury the bottom one-third—but remember which is the bottom! This method can get you twenty new plants from one blade.

ROOT CUTTINGS

To harvest root cuttings, dig the plant out, take your roots, and then replant it. To cause the least amount of disturbance to the mother plant, do this when it is at its most dormant. If the plant is too big to lift, expose one or two roots, and dig those out carefully and cut. Use two- to four-inch lengths of pencil thickness. The top cut should be flat and the bottom slanted, so you can tell the difference. The top of a root cutting is always the part that was nearest to the stems of the plant, so remember to hold all root cuttings the same way when you cut them (it is also the top part that propagates most readily). Choose only young roots and don't take more than four or five from any plant—leave some for another guerrilla, another war.

Plant the roots as soon as possible to prevent drying out. Plant about one-half to one inch below the surface, and only lightly brush soil over the top of the roots, then water. Keep the roots moist but don't overwater, as this will cause rot. Thick roots have to be planted vertically; very thin roots

---

ROOTS FOR THE REALIST

Try starting plants from root cuttings of the following:

- Acanthus
- Brambles
- Blackberry
- Daphne
- Flowering quince
- Loganberry
- Plumbago
- Raspberry
- Wisteria

Preparing a root cutting.

should be planted horizontally, parallel to the surface, and you don't have to worry about which end is up.

Where you get real winters, you can plant native roots outside in late fall, and they will have shoots in the spring. Don't transplant until the next fall, though, and then only to a pot. Keep the plant protected through the winter and plant it permanently the next spring. Or, if you don't want to take a chance, you can store the roots at 35 to 40 degrees over the winter.

And note: you can take root cuttings from perennials, even if their top growth has died in a wintery climate. Its roots are alive.

when good cuttings go bad

The reasons that a cutting doesn't make it can get pretty technical, but here goes:

AIR TEMPERATURE

When the temperature goes up, the metabolism quickens (in plants only, unfortunately—if it were true of humans, what a great alternative to dieting). This means that respiration and photosynthesis (remember eighth grade biology?) increase, but if it's too warm, respiration does so faster than photosynthesis. This makes for stunted growth and even death. And conversely, if temperatures are too low, rooting will be slow or nonexistent because the plant's metabolism will grind to a halt. Your best bet is to try to maintain the temperature of the plant's native habitat, and at most give it a bit more warmth in the soil region. Use one of a variety of devices you can buy, if you must (check at a local nursery). Don't put your plantings on the radiator, though—it's too hot.

LIGHT

Cuttings are stressed from the moment they are taken until they sprout roots. Controlling the light they get by shading them helps them to retain water without making the mistake of overwatering. A rule of thumb is to provide shade about 50 percent of the time— either naturally or with translucent cloth—like a little market umbrella. Then, as roots form (after a few weeks), gradually increase the light to induce photosynthesis. Too much light at this stage will slow root growth—and because light equals warmth, the cuttings now need a bit more warmth below and the coolish atmosphere above, which means regulated sun.

WATER

As with seeds, you do need to keep the soil around your cuttings from drying out—just a few hours of dry

---

BACK TO BASICS

Here's a tip—the easiest way in the world to grow something, as we all know from when we were kids, is to put a pit (avocado) or a tuber (potato) in a glass of water. You can actually do this with cuttings. Do it during the growing season, though, when there's lots of sunlight. You'll want to take a cutting from the tip—the youngest part, the growing part—of a stem, and keep it little, under three inches. An ideal time to do this is if you see someone pruning a tree or plant. After a few weeks, there should be plenty of roots, and you can pot your little plant, but be sure to use (at first) a potting mixture that holds lots of moisture so the water-grown roots will make the adjustment more easily. You can even try this method with hardwood cuttings like rosemary and lavender. They'll just take longer to root.

earth can kill a cutting. So your best bet is to make a cover for your baby (a plastic bag or soft drink bottle: see the previous discussion on mini-greenhouses), which will keep moisture in and also protect it from wind and downpours and excessive cold if it's outside. On the other hand, too much water causes rot, especially when cuttings are in pots.

PLANT DIVISION

Aside from uprooting a whole plant for your garden, division is the most surefire way to propagate. Be aware, however, that it is a difficult capture because it takes a bit of time, during which you might be spotted by an enemy. With that caveat, here's how to do it.

Dividing a thickly rooted plant.

dividing crowns

With this caveat, here's how to do it. Cut around the subject plant with a garden fork or a spade, and gently lift it out. Use two garden forks back-to-back to pry the plant apart, which you can then do with subsequently smaller portions. Cut connected roots, if they won't separate for you, and very tough crowns, with a sharp knife. (The crown is the part just below the surface from which new shoots arise.) Toss out the aging center. The size of each clump you're going to plant should fit into the palm of your hand. You're just splitting a plant into a number of smaller plants. This method is especially good with plants that grow outward rather than upward, as the center section tends to die back anyway. It's best done in early spring, as plants are just starting to grow and the ground is warming. By the way, you can and should use division with mature plants in your own garden, if for no other reason than to replenish the centers.

dividing rhizomes

A rhizome is the swollen part of the stem, at soil level—it's sort of between a stem and a root. Iris is the most common plant that propagates via this method, so go look at a bed of iris. In colder climates, you should lift out the plant and cut off the rhizomes, leaving a bit and some roots with the parent plant, which you can then replant. Wash all soil off the rhizome, then cut into one- to one-and-one-half inch lengths. Plant the rhizomes in a sterile medium, like perlite or vermiculite, to half their depth. Water them thoroughly and keep them warm. The following rhizomatous plants are good for guerrillas: bamboo, calla lily, ferns, iris, and water hyacinth.

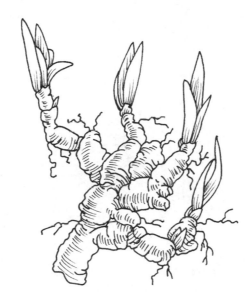

Iris rhizomes.

LAYERING

Layering happens in nature a lot—it's the way ivy spreads, and plants like blackberries and raspberries, and also plants with long, thin branches that eventually droop toward the ground or are pushed there by upper branches or even snow. If you do it yourself, all it involves is choosing a vigorous branch from low down on the plant, and putting it into the earth. Some deciduous bushes add two to three feet of new growth—which is best for this method—a year. It's a great way to propagate because the baby never leaves its mother until it's ready to—when it has roots.

To help nature along, take off all the leaves in the mid-section of a long branch, then dig a small hole where you want your new plant to grow. Bend the branch down into the hole, cover it with earth, and put a good-sized stone on top. Then bend the branch again so that the growing tip of the branch is sticking out of the ground. Tie the tip to a dowel or any stick with a supermarket twist-tie, so it continues to grow, but upright. You can try making

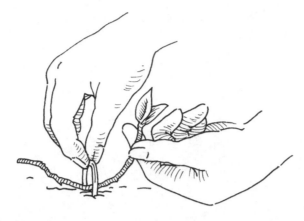

Layering a long branch.

a small cut in the part of the stem you're going to bury or scrape off a bit of bark to speed up the rooting process—but don't overdo it or the branch might snap in two. Put some rooting hormone on the injury. When rooted, cut the new plant from the mother plant and leave it where it is or transplant it. Serpentine layering is just what it sounds like: bend exceptionally long shoots to the ground in two or more places, making sure that there are leaves and buds between each buried portion and proceed as just described. Of course, to layer, you have to have captured the rooted plant first (or @#%&*? bought it).

DROPPING

I'm not particularly fond of the drop method, because it means sacrificing the entire mother plant. It's just what it sounds like. Dig up the plant, dig a much deeper hole, and drop the mother plant into it to half its height. What you get will look like a bunch of little plants. And like magic, little plantlets will root and grow from these little plants—branches of the original plant—which you can then cut from the mother plant and pot or put around your garden. This method works best with multistemmed plants—the same kind you'd propagate by division—that are young, with stems that aren't more than one–half-inch thick.

If you're trying to uproot a whole plant, (not in someone's beloved garden, please, unless you have permission), it's better to wait, if you can, until the ground is at least damp. Plants in moist soil will give up much more easily, and you won't have torn roots. Of course, it's always better to dig out the plant with enough dirt around it so that the roots aren't disturbed at all. You might not always have your weapons with you, though, or you might not have time.

RANDEL'S WAY

Randel is my gardener. He has eleven brothers and sisters, and his family came from Zacatecas in Mexico, where some of them, including Randel, have returned to build houses and grow mangoes for the market, raise money for civic purposes such as installing water pipes, find wives, and christen their babies. In the United States, they all live within a few streets of each other, except the brother who's getting a doctorate at Berkeley, and I'm really envious of the closeness of their huge family.

Anyway, Randel gives me gardening tips from Zacatecas in between our wide-ranging conversations every Friday (politics, the cost of medical care, whatever), and here are two that sound so easy I'm going to try them as soon as I get around to it.

To grow a new tree: put a baggie with earth in it around a young branch, securing it with wire or twine, keep the earth

Now that it's safely long in the past, some thirty-year-olds admitted to me that when in college they liberated Valentine's Day flowers from the graves of a nearby cemetery, thrilling their girlfriends with their uncharacteristic thoughtfulness.

moist, and in a few weeks roots will sprout in the earth. At that point you can cut the branch off the parent tree. Trim it down to about six inches, and plant.

For roses, which can be real finicky, try this: cut off a few branches, spray them with water, dip them in rooting hormone, then put them in a Ziploc bag in a dark place. They'll sprout roots super fast. Rosarians, those super-obsessed rose gardeners, probably would have no truck with this simple method.

CHAPTER FOUR

FIELD MANUAL

There's no point in going to battle only to have your prisoners fade when they get to camp. In the following examples I'll tell you what I've found out—through trial and error—about each plant I've propagated or that my comrades-in-arms in other climates have propagated. I've chosen plants for you that I know aren't too fussy in their growing habits or in the climates they like (or can be grown indoors in pots), and that for the most part are fast-growing so your garden can look like something in a year or so.

FLOWERS

Flowers, of course, are the flashy part of a garden—they're what your eye goes to immediately. They also draw beneficial insects and birds. For the most part, though, they need a lot of sun and fertilizer (but not nitrogen, which favors greenery over blooms), so you'll have to pay more attention to flowering plants than to others.

begonias

There are many varieties of begonia which account, in part, for the many ways in which to propagate them. I like my begonias because they are low-growing, with gorgeous, thick, often variegated leaves that are green above, purple below. But you can also find begonias with leaves that are chartreuse, gray, pink, maroon, white, or combinations of all of the above. I like the contrasting flowers and the plants' tendency to spread and vine. Begonia is a tropical plant that can also do well indoors, where it doesn't like a lot of sun except in winter, and it's great in hanging baskets. Begonias are immensely popular—like for African violets and roses, there are begonia societies—so you shouldn't have any problems taking a cutting or even just a few leaves from somewhere. If you're lucky, you'll even be able to extract a rhizome or two.

Because of their thick leaves, you'll be able to make leaf cuttings of some begonias. Choose healthy, big examples, and either cut off the stalk and make small cuts in the main veins on the underside, from which the new plantlets will grow, or cut the leaf into one-inch squares, making sure that each piece has a main vein. Either way, pin the prepared leaves down on the rooting medium, so the veins make contact with it. Use peat moss and keep moist. Little plantlets will appear growing out of the leaves in about six weeks, which you should lift carefully and replant in little pots in more peat moss until they're strong enough to grow on their own.

There are tuberous varieties of begonia, which you can propagate from plants that died back in winter (you just have to spot them when they're in full flower so you can go back). Dig up the dormant tubers, which are like bulbs, then rinse and dry them, dust the crowns (where the tuber meets the stems) with fungicide, and store in dry sand until the spring. Or, if you live where it's warm enough, plant them one inch deep (don't bury them) in a moist mixture of 50 percent sand, 50 percent peat moss. When the shoots sprout, cut the tuber in sections, each with a shoot and root, and dust the cuts with fungicide. Then plant singly in small pots in the same planting medium so that the top of the tuber is at soil level. Put in a humid, fairly bright place (for the warmth) until a plantlet has established itself.

Not wanting to grind the subject into the ground, as it were, I'll just tell you that you can also get baby begonias from stem cuttings, rhizomes in the varieties that have them, and seeds.

daylilies

An art dealer friend—who is notoriously cheap (she has a legendary eye for discovering new talent but loses all of her finds to more generous galleries) also has no known green thumb. She pulls daylilies up from along the road on her way to her weekend house in upstate New York, and plants them there.

Daylilies grow everywhere, and you'll find different varieties in different regions. Some daylilies are evergreen, some are dormant and need a cold period. Some thrive in a foreign climate for a couple of years and then die off. In cold climates, some keep on flowering all summer, and some, like mine, grow and flower about six times a year (I have no idea how they figure out when). So you'd do best to capture from your own environment. They are very easy to dig out—or if you have the tools with you, to divide, the preferred method of capture. They also spread beautifully, so you could put in ten or fifteen plants and have a nice little lily field in a few years, and you can continue to propagate via division in the privacy of your own yard.

geraniums

Geraniums are probably the easiest flowering plant to grow from a cutting. Just snap off a young (not flowering) branch about four inches from the growing tip. Stick it in the dirt, which ideally should be sandy, and add water. Don't let the soil dry out. To give the plant a more lush appearance, I usually put three or four cuttings in one pot, and to keep it full, I lop off the tops every so often, and plant *them*. Cuttings like dappled sunlight until they root, then they like six to eight hours of sun a day (although they don't get that much around my house) to make a lot of flowers. They prefer slightly acidic soil, and if you're really conscientious, you can fertilize them every six weeks during growing season.

In a cold climate you can pot geraniums, put them outside for half the year and inside in a sunny window the other half. My sister keeps hers this way at her summerhouse on Long Island, which she closes down for January and February. She leaves the temperature at 55 degrees so the pipes don't freeze. She gives the plants a good watering before she closes up, and covers them with a clear plastic bag so they'll retain moisture. It's even better if you cut them back to six inches when bringing them in, and in spring cut off half of the new growth before putting your geraniums outside again. Some people even plant in the ground during warmer months and then pot for the winter.

impatiens

Impatiens are so commonplace it's like owning a cocker spaniel in the fifties. They're the number one bedding plant across the United States. Even weekend gardeners are sick of their white, pink, purple, and coral sameness. They do, however, give great color in great abundance, and you don't even notice any foliage because the blooms are so thick. They grow in almost total shade, and in mild climates they're perennial and flower year-round. What more could you ask for?

Well, you could ask for the following: now you can find impatiens that are double-blossomed, which makes them look like small roses. You can find impatiens in heretofore unknown colors like yellow and orange; you can find impatiens with unusual foliage—bronze, variegated, acid green; you can find tiny impatiens for a tiny pot or an alpine garden.

If you're a novice or couldn't care less about what the garden snobs say, just snap off some shoots—you'll have to actually look for shoots without flowers—and plant in the usual cutting medium. Of course, there is no such thing as hardwood or greenwood with impatiens, so capture whenever you spot some easy prey. Untended gas station gardens are perfect war zones. Or, if you are wary, you can always buy one mother plant and grow a whole patch of impatiens from it. That will make for a pretty monotonous palette unless you sprinkle the babies among other flowers in

your garden or plan to give them away as party favors in tiny terra cotta pots.

Impatiens do need moist soil, and if you're planting rooted cuttings, beware of summer sun and heat. They like loose, fertilized soil when they grow up.

This is a great plant for a hanging basket—for instance, if your entire garden consists of a tiny apartment terrace on the north side of a low floor of a sixty-story building faced by another sixty-story building—i.e., total gloom, all the time.

irises

With gorgeous and delicately fragrant flowers, irises propagate themselves via rhizomes. The rhizomes grow half-submerged or just under the surface of the earth, so they're very easy to cut and separate. I wield a sharp blow with the pointy end of my spade. You might find a large field of them somewhere, the edges of which have grown past the owner's property (more or less) onto a DMZ (not the next-door neighbor's, but onto something that looks like an easement, or county land).

There was a wonderful stand of irises on my hillside when we moved into our house, and I used to love cutting one or two for a square white deco vase I had—kind of Japanese. But they started disappearing and I couldn't figure out why. It was my first encounter with gophers, who have been plaguing my little acre ever since. I once saw, right outside this office, a gopher emerge from his hole, encountering a bird standing just a few inches away, minding his own business. They stared at each other for a while then went their separate ways. Big Guy is the sort who carries insects outside to set them free, so warfare is not an option, and humane traps don't work—they've figured them out. I just have

had to learn by trial and error what doesn't appeal to them. Or sometimes I let my dogs run around and snuffle and dig into their holes, hoping that the disturbance will drive them into my neighbors' gardens. What I don't understand is why they don't eat the wonderfully tender roots of the weeds that sprout up every spring, preferring old, established plants.

lobelia

With its brilliant, deep purple-blue blossoms, lobelia provide graceful trailing stems in hanging pots or planters. In temperate climates, they make terrific ground cover around other smallish plants. Because they spread with abandon, you can propagate by division. A clump around ten inches in diameter would be ideal, and when you get to your own garden, you can divide that into  five or ten plants. Put them in the ground about ten to twelve inches apart and they should fill in nicely.

You can also take greenwood cuttings in summer. Cut into two-inch lengths, remove the lower leaves, and plant in the usual medium, and they should root in a couple of weeks. You'll have to keep the fledglings inside when it gets cold. Plant the next spring, and then you can forget about them.

nasturtiums

Nasturtiums are perennials in bright tones of orange, yellow, and red. They bloom year after year, and they self-propagate once they're established, running rampant during their flowering season (spring in the warm climates, summer in cold). If you want to start some, just uproot some plants and stick them in the ground, or take some cuttings and root them in water before planting. My source is a happy little bed growing by a busy roadside on indeterminate property far from anyone's house.

Nasturtiums are great in salads—they're peppery and beautiful to look at—or to decorate a heaping platter.

poppies

If you have the room, nothing is more felicitous than a field, preferably on a slight slope, of bright red Oriental poppies swaying in the breeze. Once you've prepared the soil of this huge (imaginary) field, a slightly backbreaking job, you can multiply an existing clump to fill it.

To propagate poppies, dig up an outer-edge clump of someone else's poppy field. Tease the roots and stems apart, and don't worry about breakage. With a clean, sharp knife, slice off where the stem meets the root with a straight cut, to remind you that this is the top of the root. Cut each root into pieces three to four inches long, making slanted cuts at the bottom of each piece (even if you plant upside down the poppies will grow, but it will take longer). If you manage to get a really big clump, you can use just the top three or four inches of each root, as it will grow more easily.

Plant the root cuttings so that the tops are just buried, which will keep them damp. The cuttings will then go on to produce roots growing into the earth and buds growing up into the air,

depending on what their genes tell them to do.

You can also plant five or six root cuttings in a small pot, using a mix of 50 percent peat and 50 percent grit.

roses

Cut softwood pencil-sized branches from a rosebush, if possible using stems where the flower has died but new growth hasn't started, so that you know it's a flowering stem. Of course, you'll be cutting off the dead flower. The cuttings should be up to eight inches long and one-quarter inch in diameter, and should include at least three leaf nodes. Be sure the stems on the cutting you're choosing have at least five leaves each. Strip off all but the top stem. The injuries from stripping the leaves that will be under the earth expose the cambium layer, where rooting starts. You can help the process by lightly scraping the stem down one side, from the bottom up about an inch. Then dip in fungicide and rooting hormone. Plant them (remember which side is up by cutting the bottom at a slant) four inches deep in sandy soil (half peat moss, half coarse sand), in partial shade. Keep the soil moist. Roots will form in a few weeks, and you should actually have flowers in the late spring. You can keep the cuttings covered with jars or plastic bottles for the first couple of weeks, but you don't have to. Transfer out of doors when the weather warms up a bit, and when established put in the ground in a very sunny spot.

If you're only getting around to capturing late in the growing season, you can also get roses from hardwood cuttings. Take three-inch lengths and plant indoors in coarse sand and peat moss. Keep the cuttings moist and under plastic cover in dappled sunlight, with bottom heat if possible, and they will be rooted and ready to plant in the spring.

Ramblers and climbers root best, but they won't last as long as bushes, although one of the most beautiful roses I ever saw was a climber in the courtyard of my in-laws' Rome apartment. It grew from the ground to a height of about twenty feet, and then stretched, on a slightly sagging supporting rope, about thirty feet across the wall. It had small yellow blooms, and once upon a time I knew what it was called. It definitely was ancient.

When you're looking for cuttings, don't use suckers, which you'll see growing like long straggly branches from the base of the bush. They won't give you the same rose as you see growing, because they're coming from the rootstock, which is what was used for grafting—most roses nowadays are hybrids.

Roses are usually coddled and nurtured by their owners, so I wouldn't just make a foray into someone's garden. Ask a friend (so many people grow roses) or look for those indeterminate situations (an empty house with an ancient For Sale sign, for instance). Or at the most, buy a real healthy-looking bush and take cuttings off it. Forget about roses if you'd have to grow them indoors—it doesn't work.

As you might imagine, there are rose-crazy gardeners—rosarians—all over the country. One group—actually maybe just two ladies working anonymously in some backwater—offered an unusual way to plant rose cuttings, which should actually work for any cuttings. I like it because you don't have to move the plantlets once they've rooted. It's a one-step deal, but in cold climates it has to be done at the start of the growing season. Here it is: prepare your cuttings as just described. Cultivate and amend the

soil in your garden where you want rosebushes. Grab a broom, turn it upside down, and push it into the earth a little deeper than the length of your cuttings. Put the cutting in that hole, with the top set of leaves aboveground. While steadying the cutting, pour coarse sand around and under it. Moisten the soil and the sand, and if it still gets brisk outside, pile some mulch around the cutting,

about one inch away from the stem to prevent rotting. Use the large plastic soft drink bottle or a glass jar method over the cutting, put mulch around it too, and if it's in direct sunlight make some shade over it (you can paint the top third of the bottle). Keep the bottle there until it's nearly stuffed with new leaves. After about a week or two, start removing the bottle gradually to acclimate the cutting to the outside. With this method, when roots form, they'll grow through the rooting medium—the sand—into their permanent soil! That's it.

scented geraniums

I have even more success with scented geraniums than I do with the generic, unscented kind. Among my favorites are the rose-, mint-, nutmeg-, and lemon-scented varieties. They're also a bit more delicate in appearance, and their velvety leaves (some tiny—one inch across) are beautiful. They spread in pots or in the ground, growing quickly to three feet in diameter. Their flowers are tiny, too.

Scented geraniums are more challenging to find than ordinary ones, so if you think you've spotted one at a friend's house, when no one's looking, rub a leaf between your fingers and sniff the air. Then you can snap off a piece, or ask, if you're the guilty type.

HERBS

Herbs are the workhorses in the garden: some of them produce pretty, although tiny flowers; they smell good when you brush against them; and they spread rapidly. Of course, you can also use them in cooking.

lavender

Ever since I started growing lavender, I've had the suspicion that what you smell in soaps and the like is doctored. Lavender in nature is much more pungent, much sharper than the "commercial" aroma. Still, it smells nice when you brush against it. I have big bushes of it lining one of the paths in my little front garden, although not nearly as big as those of my famous garden designer friend, which had to be a good three feet across when they were only about six months old. I'm sure that she drowned them in some super growth hormone or something.

To propagate lavender, use greenwood cuttings about four inches long, cutting below a node, and be sure to strip the leaves that will go into the earth. As with many herbs, lavender is a clumper, so you can partially dig up the plant and cut off a clump from the outer edge or tease it free with garden forks and replant your new plant. When your plant gets older, it will die out in the middle, so you'll have to cut it into clumps anyway to bring it back to its original fullness.

If you want to take hardwood cuttings, cut off flowering stems, but not too far because rooting doesn't do well with old wood. Trimming flowers will encourage the growth of new stems, which you can then harvest. If you live where it's cold, keep the cuttings in a frost-free environment until you can plant out.

mint

Mint spreads wildly and loves water. You can find it growing at the edge of streams or under a dripping outdoor faucet. Grow it from a little plant with roots. I've found that it gets root-bound very quickly in pots (probably all of that water) and doesn't thrive, so it's better in the ground. If you have no choice, you'll have to uproot the plants every once in a while and cut back the roots before repotting.

rosemary

Before I started growing my own rosemary, I used to harvest sprigs from the front of a house nearby, where it was used as a ground cover along the entire length of the property. I especially like to use it when sautéing chicken breasts in olive oil. Now all I have to do is step outside my door.

You can grow rosemary by taking greenwood cuttings from new growth. Plant the cuttings in a mixture of peat and coarse sand, and spray them with water every morning and afternoon the first week. Or you can try division, or once you have an established plant, layering.

Rosemary gets very woody and really does need to be cut back frequently, so if you get tired of rosemary in everything you cook, you can use it in flower arrangements, or tie sprigs of it to gifts, or grow little plants from cuttings as party favors.

watercress

Watercress grows in and around streams, and if you're lucky enough to have a little brooklet in your backyard, great. It looks beautiful in its natural setting. If you don't have a waterscape, you can pot it or grow it in a bed, but then think of it as food and not an ornamental. The easiest way to grow it is to pull out little plantlets and replant where you want them.

VINES

I've included some vines because they're easy to propagate once you have a plant growing (via layering) and they cover a lot of ground—or a wall—rapidly.

blackberry

My friend Dagny has a cattle ranch three hours north of where I live. It would be overrun with blackberry thickets if it weren't for the constant clearing by bulldozer that her ranch hands have to do. A few years ago, after I collected about two gallons of berries to take home—in about ten minutes—I decided it would be great to have my own bushes. Warning: they are impossible for a normal person to dig out. One of the hands had to do it for me, with a sharp knife, a sharp-edged shovel, and a lot of muscle.

Once you wrestle a plant free, just stick it back in the ground wherever you want it to grow—only don't put it near anything you cherish because that plant will get smothered by aggressive berry love. Many berries spread by putting out runners (trailing stems) that will root. Cut back the runners to six inches so the plant's energy will go into the roots. The plants will go dormant in the winter.

If you don't like where they're headed, pull the runners up (gently) with the roots and redirect. The runners, or canes, are biennial. The first year they grow and also produce side branches, and the second year they bear fruit. If you don't have a lot of room, you can train the canes on a trellis against a sunny wall. After the harvest, cut off all the old canes that have borne fruit.

Berries are outdoor plants only, and anyway you wouldn't like to get nailed by one of their unbelievably thorny runners every time you walk by the coffee table. My gardener has to use double leather gloves to deal with them. (Forewarned is forearmed.)

It's a testament to the quality of my soil that it's taken four years for these marauders to even start to spread on my hillside. Given the thick tenacity of their roots, however, they should hold it back way better than the forty-year-old pine up there. Berries: so far, sparse, or the animals get them first, plus it's too steep and I'm too lazy to check them out every other day.

clematis

Clematis is a vine that bears spectacular flowers. There are more than two hundred varieties, so you're bound to find one you like. Like almost all flowering plants, clematis wants lots of sun. And it needs something to grow on—a trellis or an uneven wall or a column that supports your roof overhang would all work. Clematis needs fast-draining soil that is slightly acidic, a condition you can achieve with an addition of peat moss. The roots have to be kept cool—in the shade, or under mulch or a ground cover. When the babies are being planted out, you have to be sure to give them little stakes to start their climbing on—the stems are fragile.

Grow clematis from softwood cuttings, taken in spring or early summer. Each cutting should have a well-formed leaf bud. Cut leaves (there should be about three of them) in half, or if you've got a particularly large-leafed specimen, leave only one leaf on your cutting. Dip in fungicide and rooting hormone and plant

in a mixture of 50 percent sand, 50 percent peat moss. Bottom heat isn't necessary.

If you already have one growing, you can also propagate clematis via serpentine layering. Just choose a long, healthy vine, make slight nicks every sixteen inches or so with a clean knife to facilitate rooting, and press down into the soil. Secure with plastic bag ties bent into croquet-hoop shapes so the vine doesn't pop up; you can remove these when the vine has rooted.

ivy

Ivy spreads so easily because it sprouts roots wherever a shoot comes in contact with the ground. If ivy is already growing on your little acre, you can facilitate this process by gently pressing down on the shoot and securing it at short intervals with a plastic bag twist-tie bent into a U-shape. When the ivy is rooted,

remove the twist-tie. If you need to appropriate your ivy from scratch, make cuttings with one leaf each (and snip off half of the leaf to push energy into rooting). Snip off the cuttings just below a leaf node. Plant in well-draining soil, in dappled sunlight, and don't let your cuttings dry out.

Note that if you live on a hill, like I do, you'll find that your groundcovers grow downhill. They eventually die out where you planted them, and start growing at the other end, into your downhill neighbor's yard. You have to start cuttings from this newest growth and replant at the top to keep the conveyor belt moving.

passionflower

I have a friend who's a fabric designer, and last time I saw her she had dried some passionflowers in her microwave as an experiment, and in fact they kept their color and were absolutely beautiful, much brighter than pressed flowers. She was going to use them for inspiration. I have to try it, too.

Passionflower is a vine that produces gorgeous blooms, comes in many different varieties, and bears delicious fruit. You can propagate it via softwood or greenwood cuttings. Place the cuttings in a mixture of peat moss and coarse sand. If you have continued access to a plant, you can try your hand at layering or serpentine layering, because this plant makes very long shoots. And, if you have no other choice, you can harvest some seeds, which have a hard coat, so you'll have to soak them for twenty-four hours in hot water. (I'm not sure I'd get up the few times in the middle of the night necessary to it keep it hot enough—those days are long gone for me.)

In cold climates, passionflower is for the most part a house-plant, although there are one or two varieties that are winter hardy, dying back and then resprouting in the spring. If you live where winters occasionally get cold, put your passionflower vine in a protected area, like against a sunny garage wall and away from cold winds, and mulch well.

BUSHES AND FLOWERING BUSHES

Bushes might not be the most exotic planting in your garden, but they're great for creating barriers and borders, and if they bear flowers, which many of the following do, so much the better.

acanthus

My first job at Sotheby's was editing the auction catalogues. Over and over again, I would read, re: eighteenth- and nineteenth-century furniture, *decorated with acanthus leaf molding*. I knew how to spell the word, but never had an idea of what an acanthus leaf looked like until years later when I started taking an interest in gardening. (Obviously, ornate old furniture was not my thing, or I would have gone downstairs to the presale exhibitions to check things out.) This is what they are: big (up to two feet long), shiny, dark green, deeply lobed leaves, which grow on clumping stalks two to three feet high and which make an excellent background for smaller flowering plants, grasses, and succulents. Flowers are on spikes, in lilac, white, pink, or green. Acanthus are fierce spreaders, with roots traveling underground all over the place—which isn't all bad. If you just want acanthus for the foliage, you can cut off the flower stalks before they bloom.

Acanthus like moist, shady conditions, but they're adaptable and can also grow where it's sunny and dry, with the right care.

Because they're clumpers, you can propagate acanthus by division. (But don't wait until the fall to do this if you live where it gets cold and wet.) You can also make root cuttings. Dig up the plant gently, wash it off, and cut off no more than one-third of the strongest, thickest roots from the parent plants. Cut each root into three-inch pieces, with an angled cut at the bottom so you remember which way to plant the root. Dip the root sections in fungicide, make holes in your planting medium with a skewer, and insert the root cuttings with the tops even with the soil surface. Top off with coarse sand and water, and keep in a sheltered place. You will see shoots before roots form, so don't transplant until you're sure you have roots.

angel's trumpet

Angel's trumpets are the gorgeous flowers you see in paintings by Georgia O'Keeffe, only she called them jimsonweed, and they're as poisonous as they are beautiful. Their botanical name is *Datura* or *Brugmansia*—I looked into this because I was getting a different story from every so-called expert I asked, and now I'm throwing all four names at you so you can figure it out. Anyway, you won't need a name if you see angel's trumpet in flower—huge (seven- to ten-inch) blossoms hanging down from a light green-leafed bush like a choir of bells. The big, deco-like flowers are wonderful when they're bathed in moonlight, and nighttime is when they release their subtle perfume, so you'll want to have a bush on the patio for romantic evenings. It's a must for a moonlight garden.

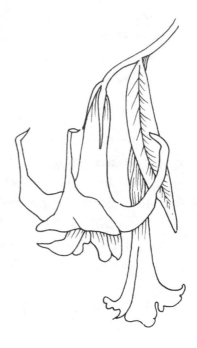

The best way to grow angel's trumpet is from cuttings. The wood of this shrub never really hardens off—it really is kind of like a weed—so you'll have to take softwood or greenwood cuttings, four to six inches long, with no bud or flower, of course. Because the leaves get really huge, get rid of all but one whole one, or a couple that you've cut in half, and plant in a free-draining soil, that is, lots of sand or if you use potting soil, a lot of vermiculite or perlite. If you live in a cold climate, you're not going to have much of a plant before winter rears its head, so you'll definitely have to baby it inside. And, if you live in a cold climate and see this beauty when you're away from home, making it inconvenient to carry cuttings (through Customs, say), you can also propagate from seeds, planting them in early spring. Keep the young plants warm by covering them with a plastic sheet.

Angel's trumpet is tropical. Although it grows well outside in temperate climates, and it can actually stand some frost in winter, it would be much happier inside in a colder climate, with not much of either water or sun. It grows as a large shrub, which you can train into a tree, but I wouldn't start the branches too high up or the flower's drama will be out of reach. The most common angel's trumpets are white, but I've also seen yellow and occasionally orange-red ones.

azalea

Azalea bushes are another overly enthusiastic producer of blooms, like impatiens, and they've also become commonplace, like impatiens. But they are pretty, come in many colors, and if you're a novice you've probably never noticed them anyway. My husband bought me a supermarket plant for Mother's Day about fifteen years ago, and it's still going strong. I've never taken cuttings from it because (1) I don't like supermarket plants (sorry, Big Guy) and (2) Having been a sort of gardener for so long, I've grown to like more unusual plants. One thing to remember: azaleas are a type of rhododendron, and as such they really like acidic, nondry soil.

If the mother plant is deciduous, take softwood cuttings from new growth, but then cut off the soft tip to prevent rotting. Prune the plant shortly after the cutting takes root, to ensure that it doesn't grow straight up, but instead becomes nice and bushy. Cuttings should be two or three inches long, with one or two pairs of leaves, and if they're real big, cut them in half. Dip the cuttings in root toner and use a skewer or a stick to make the insertion hole. The planting medium should be equal parts peat

and perlite. Keep azaleas in a warmish, moist place with protection from really hot sun; in a harsh climate, be prepared to protect them the first winter with mulch and a clear plastic cover, in a corner of your garden that the wind misses.

If you're borrowing from an evergreen azalea, take greenwood cuttings and proceed as just described.

bamboo

My favorite bamboo garden ever is a block from the ocean in eastern Long Island. Like palms, bamboo can grow in cold climates (to 20 degrees below zero!) where you'd never expect to find it. This stand, in a famous garden, is about thirty feet high, and it's designed as an allée—a long, narrow pathway—leading to a round "room," enclosed by the bamboo, where we had a picnic. A secret garden, a magical place.

Bamboo is a notorious spreader. When you don't want it to, it will pop up in the weirdest places. I've found it on my terrace between bricks and under the deck twenty feet away from the original clump, growing through the knot holes in the wood. But I've also managed to get it to grow between the deck and the garage wall, which has made a great privacy screen when I want to dry my hair in the sun. If you're just beginning to grow it, its voracious spreading quality is a big plus.

There are two ways to propagate bamboo. The first is to dig up a clump, including a large root ball, and move it to its new home. Wait until autumn when the growing season is over and try to get a clump at least two feet in diameter, with three or four plants. Bamboo spreads by rhizomes, and they are famously tough—you'll need a sharp shovel or a saw to free them from the mother plant. And very important: although bamboos are extremely hardy, once uprooted they can't be allowed to dry out for even a few minutes. So if you're not transplanting immediately, water the roots and leaves and wrap them in plastic right away. Before you plant your clump, cut back the canes to twelve inches to reduce water loss, and dip the cut root and rhizome surfaces in fungicide—this is especially important if you only manage to get some baby rootlets with shoots that you're going to plant first in pots. Bamboos need water, so don't rake up fallen leaves at the plant base once you've planted it out. The leaves will retain water, and they also contain silica that your bamboo

specifically needs—it's also what makes the leaves sharp enough to slice your finger.

If you're eyeing a questionable source, and the aforementioned rather involved operation is not an option, you can try propagating by cutting off a cane—called a culm by bamboo fanatics, of which there are many—and cutting it into four- to six-inch pieces. (Remember the rule: cut the tops straight across and the bottoms at a slant.) Plant the canes entirely under the earth.

At my local farmers' market, there's a booth where they sell only "lucky bamboo"—black bamboo canes a few inches long that are growing in water, with a few leaves and some roots. I don't know how lucky they are, if they really grew in water, or if they'll keep on growing, but they look pretty and you could give it a try.

barberry

Barberry makes a great barrier bush, with its thorns and spiny leaves, which, I am here to tell you, are not fun to step on when you run out barefoot to get the mail. There are almost countless varieties of barberry shrubs, some deciduous, some evergreen, growing in different climates all over the country, and in all sorts of difficult soils. Most produce little yellow flowers followed by red or blue-black berries, and they make nice hedges. If you can find a pygmy, it would make a good specimen for your alpine garden—they don't grow higher than eighteen inches and you can prune them back even shorter.

Although barberry does spread via underground runners, which is a plus once you've got an established plant you'd like to see spread into a hedge, it's easier to grow from cuttings. Take lateral branches—i.e., not shoots growing straight up—of softwood

or hardwood, four to six inches long, and plant in coarse sand with bottom heat or other protection from the cold if your climate mandates it.

In some places barberry bushes are actually invasive (it's that layering, which causes them to spread) and are considered weeds. On the plus side, the berries are revered herbal remedies, and you can make delicious jam from them, too.

blueberry

Forget about blueberries if you live in a warm, dry climate with alkaline soil. This bush's requirements are just like those of rhododendron and azalea—cool, moist but well draining and acidic soil. If you live in a cool to cold climate, you can plant your rooted cuttings in pure peat moss, which will provide the acid. And to get berries, go for cuttings of different varieties, if you can. You'll eventu- 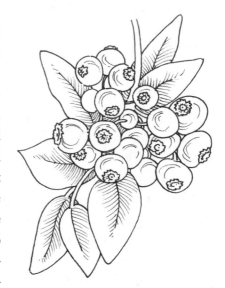 ally get as many as twenty pounds of berries per bush—which equals twenty pints. I just bought a pint at the supermarket for $2.99, and they don't taste like much. And if you can't eat them all, you can freeze them; don't wash them first. Lucky you if you can grow your own and luxuriate in real blueberry taste. The closest most of us come is blueberry pancake syrup at the local IHOP.

Anyway, take four- to six-inch greenwood cuttings in early summer, strip off all but two leaves, and dip in fungicide and rooting hormone. Plant in a mixture of 50 percent sand, 50 percent peat moss, and you should have a hardy plantlet by first frost, which you can transplant to a protected but sunny part of your garden.

broom

My English mother-in-law expressed disbelief when I told her I'd never heard of broom (or gorse as it's called in England). That's because it didn't grow where I grew up. Anyway, I love to see its bright, yellow blossoms on the hillsides around here, knowing that its strong roots will do their bit to prevent slides, and they never even ask for a drink of water. And there are tiny varieties for your alpine (read really small) garden.

To grow broom, take greenwood or hardwood cuttings. Plant them in a free-draining medium like sand with perlite. Provide the plant with some humidity but not too much water, and use fungicide and rooting hormone. These cuttings take a long time to root, so if you've got them covered with plastic be sure to ventilate them once a week so they don't rot.

butterfly bush

Butterfly bush is a great, fast-growing, flowering, fragrant shrub or small tree (depending on how you prune it), and it's found in all climates. Where it's cold, the bush freezes back to the ground but jolts back to life in the spring. It grows like a weed, even up to ten feet in a season, with huge clumps of flowers, and thrives even in terrible soil, although it needs good drainage and at least occasional watering if you live where the weather doesn't oblige.

Take softwood cuttings from a growing tip, reduce the foliage by half, and simply stick them in sand. Remember to keep your babies warmish if you live where it's cold, either with bottom heat, indoors, or in a protected area with some sun—until it stays warm out all by itself.

forsythia

Forsythia is not for your average desert landscape (forget it). I remember these bushes with their cheerful yellow blossoms as the first real sign that spring had arrived back in New Jersey. They're one of the easiest plants to root from cuttings. Cut four-inch lengths of softwood from a growing tip in June, dip them in fungicide and rooting hormone, and plant the cuttings in equal amounts of peat and perlite. If you happen to have a longer-leafed variety, strip about half of the leaves away. Provide some bottom heat if you're set up for it, otherwise keep your pots in a protected area, with, once again, dappled sunlight. If you're lucky enough to have a forsythia bush growing already, you can make new plants by layering.

fuchsia

Fuchsia's exotic-looking blossoms are way out of fashion—they're from the time of avocado and gold kitchen appliances and wall-to-wall shag. So it's just about time for them to make a comeback, and you can do your bit to help.

If all you have is a terrace off the living room of your condo, don't despair—fuchsias look great in hanging baskets or window boxes. They're really versatile, though—if you have more room, you can grow them as shrubs, trees, bushes, espaliers, topiaries, and even groundcover.

Fuchsias are some of the easiest plants to grow from cut-tings—they almost always make it, and they should actually flower the first season you plant them out. You can take cuttings anytime during the growing season. Clip cuttings with one-half inch of stem above and one-half inch below a set of leaves, then plant them in florist's foam, that spongy green stuff. Soak little cubes of the foam in water for ten to fifteen minutes so they're saturated, then place them on an old, deep dish or tray and make

a one-half-inch deep hole in each one with a small skewer. Put a cutting in each one, with the leaves just above the surface and the stem touching the bottom. Do as many as you have room for, then add one-half inch of water; put the whole thing in a plastic bag and place it in a cool and lightly shaded place. The roots will actually grow through the sponge, so you'll know when it's time to plant out, and you can just pot the whole thing, sponge and plant. Just make sure

to cover the foam with your potting soil, otherwise it will dry up and draw water away from the new roots.

The mature plant likes moist, well-draining soil, coolish temperatures, and modified sunlight. (Mine grow in the shade, although I have the feeling they'd do better with at least a little sun.) If you live where it's cold, grow fuchsias in pots that you can take inside or prepare them for winter outdoors by first cutting the plant back, and then mounding six inches of sawdust over the roots.

hibiscus

A bush with exotically beautiful blooms, hibiscus can be amazingly hardy. It doesn't grow only in Hawaii like you'd think, with those hula dancers wearing them tucked behind an ear. For cold climates, there are deciduous hibiscus that die back in winter, or you can grow them in containers and bring them indoors before the first frost. The flowers are big (four inches across) to huge (twelve inches!) and need feeding, deep watering, and mulch to keep the moisture in.

To grow, gather some strong softwood cuttings early in the growing season (remember, always without flower buds), and plant in perlite only; or in warm climates, take leafy hardwood cuttings and plant in peat moss and sand until the plants are rooted.

hosta

Hostas have wonderful leaves—shiny, wavy, heart-shaped, thick-veined in an array of colors from almost true blue to golden (to light up a dark corner), varie-gated (multicolored), and gray-white. If you have a shady yard, they'll do fine. That they make flowers—white, lavender, blue, some-times fragrant, is almost an

afterthought. They look great as a backdrop for grasses. And because they're clump formers, they're easy to propagate by division.

A hosta clump might be large and tough, in which case you'll have to divide it with a spade or shovel and elbow grease. If it's younger and looser, tease it apart gently with garden forks to minimize root damage. You can then plant out small clumps, in pots if you want, and in a year they should form another clump.

If you really want to get into it, you can also perform a little surgery on hosta buds. It's called topping. When your single buds shoot up, clean away the earth to expose the crown and make a lit-tle vertical slit in each one with a clean knife. Then dust the crown with rooting hormone and fungicide, and stick in a piece of tooth-pick to keep the wound open. Re-cover the crown and water it. New buds will eventually form around the cuts, which you can then redivide, *ad infinitum*.

If you can't find a convenient source of hosta (which means a really mature plant, as they can be slow to re-establish), you can actually buy one at a nursery and perform the division or top-ping on it, winding up with many for the price of one. It's what nurseries do; you can do it, too.

hydrangea

To start hydrangea bushes, begin with a softwood cutting with up to three pairs of leaves, and no flowers, of course. These cuttings will wilt rapidly, so be sure you have some plastic bags to put them in until you get home. Because these bushes make large, floppy leaves, you'll have to remove all but the two uppermost ones, and then you'll have to cut them in half, so that the growing energy goes to the roots. Be sure to cut off the growing tip for the same reason, and also so that you get a nice bushy plant instead of one that just gets tall.

Because softwood cuttings are delicate, first make a hole in the planting medium with a divet, and after you've dipped the cutting in fungicide and rooting hormone, drop the stem in.

peony

There's nothing more gorgeous than a vase full of heavy-headed, ripe peonies. Some are even scented. To me, they're what roses aspire to.

To propagate, divide off a clump with a sharp old knife or a spade. If you wind up with some torn roots, be sure to cut them cleanly when you get home, then treat with a fungicide. And don't let the roots dry out. If you're not going to get to them for a day or two, you can "plant" them loosely in moist peat or sterile soil.

If you have a generous aunt or neighbor who won't mind, at the end of the growing season you can cut off the stems to just below the surface of the soil, lift the entire crown (everything underground, plus small buds) of the plant, wash it off, and cut it into sections. Dip the cuts in fungicide and replant, with baby buds about one inch below the surface. You can replant some of the sections in your donor's garden and take the others for yourself. Once you've

replanted, though, don't move them because it will take a couple of years for flowers to appear.

You can also be less voracious and make root cuttings of peonies—take just a very small clump and cut off the roots. Then cut those into three-inch pieces. Cut the top end (the end nearest the plant) straight and the bottom end slanted, so you plant them right side up.

Plant in a mixture of 50 percent peat and 50 percent grit or coarse sand, being sure to cover the whole root so it stays moist.

This is another plant whose seed propagation is more trouble than it's worth. The seeds have to undergo two cold winters before they make shoots.

rhododendron

Rhododendrons can get huge; I've seen them thirty feet across. Forget trying this bush in a warm climate or a very dry one. Think England, or the Pacific northwest—they like moist soil that never dries out completely. Acidic soil is good— no deserts, which are alkaline. Don't plant rhododendrons in the sun—they like to grow in the dappled light of forests, or each other. If you've got all of this in your backyard, and you live in the right climate, it's all you need, other than a topping of compost or pine needles or bark (all of which are acidic).

Take greenwood cuttings, four inches long, and plant them in peat moss and coarse sand.

Be aware that in areas where deer abound, evergreen rhododendrons are going to get eaten up to their knees when other trees and bushes are bare. So protect young plants for a few years until they can withstand this kind of haircut.

viburnum

Viburnums grow everywhere except where it's really hot—Palm Springs, Death Valley, like that. They give you everything—flowers, berries—which bring birds—fragrance, pretty leaves. And they can take some shade. A viburnum shrub can serve as a backdrop for the rest of your garden, or it can be interwoven with other larger plants. Viburnums are deciduous, evergreen, or even partly evergreen in some climates, and most varieties can tolerate acidic or alkaline soil,

as long as they get moisture. Some varieties can grow into small trees, and the leaves of some turn interesting colors at the end of the growing season. The flowers are usually white or pink, and some make electric blue berries!

Start your viburnums from cuttings—greenwood for deciduous varieties and hardwood for evergreens. The cuttings should have three nodes and two leaves. Cut large leaves in half. If you live in a cold climate, you'll have to keep the babies indoors or, if they're rooted and well on their way, protect them under glass and with straw mulch.

After you've got a nice big bush, you can start making new viburnums by layering. If the branch you're planning on using is stiff, you'll have to dig a little trench about three inches deep, bend the branch into it, and secure it to the soil with strong wire "staples" (which you can make from a roll of wire). Then stick a wood stake in the trench, bend up the branch tip, and tie it to the stake with biodegradable string or straw. Then fill the trench and water as usual.

CACTUS AND SUCCULENTS

Cactus and succulents are the easiest kinds of plants to propagate because they carry their own water supply with them, so they don't go into shock if you miss a day or so. And they can also look exotic and weird, and make wonderful indoor plants if they don't like it outside where you live.

aloe

Light green aloe, with nonstabbing, nonspiked leaves, are truly commonplace in warm and dry climates. They're so ordinary that you even have a hard time finding them in nurseries, as though they were weeds—which is ridiculous because they're beautiful. A twenty-inch potted aloe would sell for many K-rations in New York. Aloes are easy to appropriate, since they don't bayonet and poison you like some cactus and succulents do, and their "pups" break off without a fight, often with a straggly root or two that hasn't quite managed to get itself fixed firmly in the ground yet. A huge plus with this succulent is that great big ones (I'm talking about a four-inch-wide stalk, even sawn off with no roots) will do just as well as pups when stuck in the ground. And you don't have to wait a couple of years to have a gorgeous, mature plant. Just water for a few weeks if it's not raining enough.

Because my own acre (mostly perpendicular to level ground) was full of aloes when we arrived; I didn't need to acquire them by stealth, and over the years I've planted babies and grownups everywhere. On the other hand, no one's ever asked me if they could have a couple either, but maybe they used my tactics.

Health benefits: surely you've seen aloe vera hand cream, shampoo, and so on—well, it's this plant that all that manufactured stuff comes from. So if you live where it grows or can get someone to FedEx it to you if you don't, learn how to use it. When Big Guy got a hideous sunburn in Baja California (sitting under an umbrella), and there was *nada* by way of a *farmacía* to be found, a handyman at the place where we were staying cut off some big aloe spears. He sliced them down the middle and told us to keep applying the jellylike stuff it produces. It worked. It also turns bloody red and begins to stink like rotten meat after a few hours, so there must be something really weird in there.

blue agave

To grow blue agave, just stick a fledgling in the ground, prefer-ably with some roots, and water it for a while, unless it's raining. You can grow your plant indoors, but it will eventually get too enormous to keep, like an adorable bear cub who grows up.

This is the plant that gives us tequila, and real tequila is made only from blue agaves. Blue agaves grow on plantations, and like French wine can only bear the designation if they are grown in the government-outlined area of Mexico near the town of Tequila, in the state of Jalisco. In the past few years, trendy restaurants and wine stores have started offering selections of as many as 150 dif-ferent tequilas, and they can get very pricey. You can use less expensive brands in cooking, especially with fish and pork. Warn-ing: do not try harvesting blue agaves around Tequila. Because of the huge demand in the United States, prices for unprocessed agave have gone way up and locals have been stealing the plants. The Mexican police are on to them, and arrests are happening. Seven years in a Mexican jail is not a pleasant prospect.

Some "experts" contend that blue agaves are members of the lily family; others that they're succulents. It doesn't matter. What they are is gorgeous. They get real big (there's one that's six feet across on my block), and my gardener (you remember Randel) says they're very expensive to buy in a nursery (I wouldn't know). They are extremely thick-leaved and spiky, and at least at the two stands (on very busy streets) that I've tried to cruise by slowly, the pups aren't plentiful or well-formed, and are stuck really close to the big, dangerous mothas, like baby warthogs on the savannah. But I was determined to have one.

The other day I drove by some men installing a fence in front of someone's house; they had uprooted about eight blue agaves. I rang the doorbell, no one home. When I returned an hour later, they told me the owner said I could have the plants. I paid the crew $20 to drive the agaves to my house, and they dumped them off in the driveway; nothing could get them to bring them up the stairs. I soon realized why—the biggest one weighed about 250 pounds, as my gardener Randel and two helpers soon found out when they had to lug them up my hill. To lighten their load, I sawed off damaged spikes, wearing shorts, a T-shirt, and flip-flops. Their juice is worse than poison ivy and poison oak. I thought I would scream with the itching; I ran in, showered, and slathered myself with extra-strength Benadryl cream. Three weeks later I still had actual scars from the rash. They make tequila out of this stuff by cooking it. Never eat raw agave—it really is poisonous.

euphorbia

Because euphorbia can have a milky sap that's really irritating and even poisonous in some species, it's supposed to repel gophers and moles, which might be true. But I've never had any success in this department excepting when I let my dogs run riot all over my mini-acre, which usually does more damage than any underground creatures do. I guess the pounding paws accomplish what those expensive battery-operated gadgets, which vibrate every thirty seconds, are supposed to do but in fact don't (I've tried), because the burrowers catch on really quick to the fact that regularity equals harmless machine. Anyway, you're welcome to try euphorbia, as I will when I get around to it.

You, however, will know this plant by its most famous variety, poinsettia. The red "flowers" are actually bracts—like those of bougainvillea—and the real flowers are the tiny white growths in the center. Although I've seen outdoor bushes eight feet high, we all know poinsettia best as the holiday plant we buy in the supermarket. Instead of watching it slowly pine away in January, you can make it thrive and even clone itself. Keep it in a sunny window;

keep the soil moist but don't let water stand in the liner. When the leaves and bracts fall, cut the plant back to two buds, reduce watering, and keep it in a cool place until late spring. Then put it outside. You can start new plants from a grownup one by taking cuttings with four or five leaf joints.

Euphorbia varieties are mind-boggling. They can have chartreuse, yellow, orange, pink, lime green, and red flowers or bracts, and one variety, the baseball plant, actually does look

135

just like a baseball. Some euphorbia have leaves that turn from green to white, making a good background for bright flowers. Note that some varieties have thorns, so gloves are a good idea.

If you're taking a cutting from a euphorbia that has that irritating sap, stand it up for an hour or so to let it drain and dry up before planting. If you're propagating a succulent euphorbia, you'll be doing it by breaking off a plantlet, thus releasing the awful sap. If you get it on your fingers, soap and water will take it off. Water alone will harden it, so you should spray the parent and dip the plantlet in plain water to stop the flow.

After you've drained the sap, plant regular cuttings in a mix of coarse sand and peat, and be sure they don't get too much moisture, which can cause rot. The mature plant can thrive in a near-desert environment.

For regular division of clumping euphorbia, try it after the plant has flowered. To put distance between yourself and the sap, wear gloves and use a spade, and remove only enough of the mother plant so that it won't suffer. You can also try "topping" (single bud division that I explain in the discussion of hosta) if you're really getting into all of this.

ice plant

Propagating ice plant is easy. Just snip off lengths eight to twenty inches long and plant them. Water the cuttings for a couple of weeks if it's not raining. If you live in a cool or cold climate, you can plant the cuttings in pots. They'll trail over the rims and look lush with very little effort.

My favorite source for ice plants: an empty lot for sale on my Aunt Emma's super-exclusive Newport Beach island. (I happen to know the owner, a big art collector, so I have a weak excuse if I ever get questioned.)

Ice plants aren't too exciting to southern Californians, as they're to be found everywhere along the sloping sides of freeways; but they're easy to retrieve, are very hardy (it has sometimes been weeks before I got around to sticking one in the ground), and grow fairly quickly. They do not put down deep roots, however, and are best used as a temporary cover, to be interspersed later with other plants as you find them.

Fellow guerrillas, remember—there are three reasons not to stop on freeway shoulders: cops are ubiquitous; some do-gooder could call 911 on her car phone; you would make an interesting drive-by target.

jade plant

You know jade plants—if you live in an old city, you usually see them in the windows of Chinese laundries; they're dusty, neglected, and there's something prehistoric about the way they look, especially as they get older and their trunks thicken. They have small, plump, dark green leaves, tiny white flowers once or twice a year, and light brown branches.

Jade plants are practically indestructible, and you can snap a small branch off the mother plant and leave it lying around for months before getting it in the ground. I do it whenever I see a bare spot that doesn't get reached by my fairly haphazard sprinkler system. They do need water at least once a month in really hot, dry weather. My mother takes small sprigs back east with her whenever she visits, and she puts them in pots in her kitchen window.

When your jade "tree" gets to be about two feet high, which happens really fast, you can start pruning it to resemble a crooked-trunked branching tree, with puffs of leaves at the ends of the branches—an ersatz bonsai. It looks great potted in a big faux-oriental jardiniere where you can grow it inside or outside.

For this plant, you really don't need special earth, root toner, or anything—just a little water and a little sun.

prickly pear

Break off a "leaf" or paddle of a prickly pear, let it dry out for a couple of days as you would with any cactus, and plant it in a pot. Water your cutting twice a week in hot weather, less in cool. You can move it into the ground when the plant is established (you should have four or five paddles), if you live in the proper climate. Or, to prevent the very real possibility of rotting, instead of putting the paddle into the earth, just lay it on top. Don't

water it, and be patient. You can start to mist it when it forms baby roots. Wear gloves when handling any part of this plant. The spikes are very sharp.

These succulents are weirdly beautiful, and their fruit is fabulous, but they're expensive if you have to buy them. I've seen different varieties, but my favorite is one at my dogs' kennel deep in the Santa Monica mountains, off a dirt road. In fact, the owner told me how to get the horrible tiny spines off the fruit with a method I've never seen suggested anywhere else—you just singe them off over a gas flame (of course, you then have to peel them before eating). When I'd take my dogs up there, I would bring along a pair of thick gardening gloves and a box, and harvest— she had a plant that was about twenty-five feet across! Alas, the last time I went there, the plant had been replaced by a huge feed shed, and I tried to smile in commiseration as she lamented that it cost $1,000 to get the damn thing out of the ground. I did notice a new stand nearby, however. I hope it manages to avoid her notice.

By the way, if you get those horrible tiny spines in your fingers, you can remove them with duct tape.

striped agave

Striped, or variegated agaves, are a good plant for the beginning gardener. Just stick them in the ground and water them if there's no rain. Or you can pot striped agaves and keep them in the sun indoors. They're not symmetrical like blue agave, but are striking, with curving, undulating spikes that are light green and ivory. The pups are pretty easy to kidnap, but you do need a shovel (not a spade) and clippers. My source is on a fairly busy road, but it's a thick stand so I try to forage deep into it, more or less hidden from disapproving commuters. The juice does not cause a rash.

Not long ago, I screeched to a stop when I saw the Bureau of Street Maintenance guys chopping down these beauties—some sort of brush fire preventive measure—though never touching the really flammable dead grass across the road. Furious, I nonetheless put on a smile and asked if I could have a few whole plants. They were very accommodating and gave me five big ones, even loading them into my Land Cruiser for me. Perfect timing.

TREES

Obviously, trees are going to take a while to look like anything in your garden (unless you're making a bonsai or otherwise growing one in a pot), but once you have a mature tree you've really got something special—unless you move around a lot in which case someone else will be enjoying it. My list is a bit eccentric, but it's meant to provide you with ideas for trees that will grow indoors or outdoors without too much fuss.

conifers

All pines are conifers, but not all conifers are pines—conifer means cone-bearing. And they're commonly called evergreens, although a few are actually deciduous, just to confuse you. The most common of these trees and bushes are cedars, cypress, fir, hemlock, juniper, larches, pine, redwood, spruce, and yews.

Grow conifers from greenwood or hardwood cuttings from the current year's growth, taken from a young tree—they will root much more easily—and don't take stems with berries or fruits. If you want a tree (a plant that grows vertically), you have to use a shoot that is growing that way: the "leading" shoot. If you want a bush, take a shoot from lower down, one that's growing sideways. The latter is especially useful if you want to grow a long hedge, as you'll have a bunch of identical bushes. The reason for this oddity is genetic—each part of the tree has different genes switched on. Some cuttings will even make dwarf varieties.

Your cuttings should be four to six inches long, slicing just below a node. You can strip off side shoots or needles from the bottom part of the cutting, which will be under the earth—the little wounds this makes will encourage rooting. The foliage that is left should not touch the earth. With a narrow skewer, make a hole in the planting medium. Dip the stem in rooting hormone and plant each section in a separate pot or put five or six together in a larger pot. Your planting medium should be one-third perlite,

141

one-third peat, and one-third finely shredded bark, or you can mix all of the above with sand, so that the medium contains 25 percent of each. Cover your babies with plastic and put them in a semi-shaded spot, but don't leave them outside if you have cold winters. Water lightly and check weekly to make sure they're not drying out, especially if you've put some heating apparatus under the soil. Once your cuttings have rooted, you can transfer them to individual containers, fertilize, and put them in moderate sunlight. When they become little trees, you can put them in the ground if they're suited to your climate.

Because these trees and bushes can get huge, be sure to look at the mother tree to make sure your landscape can accommodate your cutting when it grows up. Not all varieties can be trained to make good shrubs, windbreaks, screens, or hedges, depending on how you prune them. There are slow-growing and dwarf pines that are perfect for alpine gardens or containers.

Growing conifers from seeds is iffy, messy, and complicated. It's best, in the case of pines that have them, to just extract the seeds from the cones for use in cooking (called pinoli, piñon, or pine nuts, depending on which language you speak) and forget about planting them unless you have no choice. But if you have collected seeds, and just in case a giant asteroid hits the earth and you're one of the few survivors, the seeds will last for twenty years—so you can store them in your fridge if you have the gas to run a generator to make electricity, then plant them when things settle down.

Occasionally you'll be lucky enough to spot a seedling, which you can carefully extract from the ground. My neighbor had a lovely little tree that I've watched grow from birth, the baby of a huge old tree up the hill. It got to be about two feet high, and then her gardener lopped it off, breaking my heart. She's a friend and she knew the treelet was there (we talked about it), so I just lusted after it, but I sure would have kidnapped it if I had known what was going to happen. But surprise of surprises, it's started to grow back—it's about a foot high now. I feel like putting a little fence around it.

This is a huge subgroup of trees, which grow in as many different climates as the planet can offer below the tree line and excluding the poles. In the United States, conifers are native to the semi-desert of southern California, the perpetually rainy Pacific northwest, and the sub-zero winters of the northeast. You're not likely to have luck with exotic conifers. Don't try to grow a redwood, for instance, if you live anywhere other than where they grow naturally unless you are prepared to make a bonsai out of it.

I've found that too much water makes a pine unattractively tall and spindly. I planted a seedling much too close to a sprinkler on my hill, and it's now about ten feet high, and that's it: one ten-foot-high spindly trunk with some needles growing out of it (okay, and about two branches).

Sometimes people who buy live Christmas trees actually throw them away—I thought the whole idea was to plant them in your garden afterward. Anyway, keep your eye out for them out on the curb with all the torn holiday wrappings and the big computer cartons starting December 26.

Finally, if you can actually get your paws on a branch of giant sequoia without breaking the law and your neck, go for it. Maybe you can salvage one from a very recently fallen tree. Obviously, they grow only where they grow, in northern California, but you could make a clumsy attempt at a bonsai. And they have been propagated in laboratories in Berkeley from two-hundred-year-old trees!

Anyway, if you can get it, you need a lateral branch for your cutting, which should be six inches long. Don't worry about whether it's soft, green, or hardwood. Strip the needles from the bottom inch of the cutting, dip it in fungicide and rooting hormone, and plant it in peat and perlite. Good luck.

By the way, I just saw a tour of a giant redwood forest on PBS, and you can actually buy little redwood seedlings if you go to northern California. Maybe the same arrangement exists for giant sequoias—I'll have to find out.

crape myrtle

There are two crape myrtles in my garden, and they self-propagate by sending up shoots, about ten little plants a season. I have to start giving them away. Do for others what I have done to them.

If you don't have this situation, use greenwood cuttings, planted in peat moss and sand.

These are really bushes (they're deciduous, and their bare white bark is beautiful in winter), but you can train them to become trees, which never reach a height of more than fifteen to eighteen feet. The fuchsia or white flowers wilt and lose their color immediately if you try to use them in an arrangement, so just enjoy them on the tree—where they have a short flowering period of about two weeks. To keep them blooming profusely, you have to prune off last year's flowering wood before spring.

Crape myrtles need lots and lots of full sun, and not much water, at least where I live. The ones I see on the sidewalk medians in commercial areas in the broiling hot San Fernando Valley are the best examples, and they get no care at all. On the other hand, they seem to proliferate in the south, which means lots of natural humidity, so who knows. They can grow almost anywhere, even tolerating temperatures of 10 to 20 degrees below zero. In my sister's neighborhood in Oklahoma, where it gets mighty cold in the winter, I've seen a number of them thriving.

dwarf juniper

There is actually a real low-growing variety of this pretty ugly plant, which makes an almost impermeable ground cover. It never gets more than two inches high and is pale green-blue.

Because it's so miniature, it's also a candidate for your alpine garden.

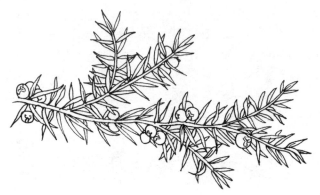

fig

Fig trees grow everywhere, but are deciduous in cold climates. I have a dwarf in a big pot that kept its leaves its first two winters but loses them now (in southern California). If you take hardwood cuttings, be sure to winterize them in cold climates. You can grow figs from greenwood cuttings too.

If you locate a big tree with long branches, you can layer the low-growing ones, providing, of course, you have permission from the owner of the tree, who might otherwise come along someday, wonder what on earth is going on when he sees your little surgery, and put an end to the whole process.

The obvious plus of growing a fig tree is having a supply of its delicious and very expensive fruit. I have an ongoing battle with the birds, however—they sink their beaks into a just-ripe fig literally the morning I'm going to pick it, making neat little circles and rendering my precious fruit inedible, although I have secretly sometimes cut around their surgery and eaten what was left. Probably not a good idea. This past summer, though, I finally

beat them to the punch: I tied little baggies around each and every fruit before it was ripe. Not too hard, because my tree is a potted miniature.

And I've found a great source—a beautiful ancient tree on an empty lot that was for sale but has been taken off the market (asking too much, I think). Anyway, I spotted the tree in the spring, went back in early August, almost too late, and, holding my baby granddaughter in one arm, pulled off as many figs as would fit in my purse with the other hand.

The big (Adam and Eve used them) leaves are decorative on a summer lunch table, or for lining a tray of cheeses.

gingko biloba

From the ancient Gingko biloba tree comes, of course, one of the latest natural wonder remedies—this one for failing brain power. I'm reminded of when, a good twenty years ago, my secretary bought me some herbal remedy that was hot back then for the same thing. She was only half-joking. Anyway, I wouldn't suggest that you start a pharmacy in your garage, but I have always loved the look of gingkos, growing unheralded (up until now) on New York sidewalks, and maybe you will too.

Only take cuttings from male trees if you have a choice, and if you can tell. You'll know why if you encounter a female that is bearing fruit, which is smelly and messy and profuse. Most street and landscape trees are, of course, going to be male for this very reason, so you should be safe. Take softwood cuttings in early summer, six- to eight-inch growing tips, and plant them in peat, perlite, and sand. You can even toss in some Styrofoam peanuts for water retention.

loquat

Loquat trees produce a luscious fruit. In the forties loquats were wildly popular, but then they disappeared. You couldn't find them anywhere, because even touching them lightly can bruise them—which would never do on a supermarket shelf with its shiny, rock-hard, perfect-looking fruit. Now, though, with the advent of farmers' markets, they've started showing up again. I'd never  heard of loquat, until Big Guy, who grew up in Rome, started talking about *nespole* and how he missed them. I had no idea what he was talking about until on one of my walks I plucked a few from a tree laden with them (they were just falling on the ground, there were so many) and brought them home. He was in heaven. I started noticing them all over, the fruit always neglected. Then I happened to look down my hill one day and there was a mature loquat tree, obviously seeded without my help because it definitely wasn't there ten years ago. It hasn't borne fruit, though, and someday I'll find out why—not enough sun? A male tree?

Because loquat trees are so hardy, growing without any attention at all, I think planting cuttings ought to work well. I did collect seeds a few months ago, but when I looked at them just the other day, they were starting to shrivel (no time to plant them, writing this book!). I did read somewhere that loquats from seeds often don't do as well as those from cuttings. If you don't live in a temperate climate, you could try it as an indoor plant. And if it won't bear fruit, its long, dark green leaves would still make a great potted plant.

moringa

I recently heard about this amazing tree and thought that you should know about it, because in its natural state the moringa is a major argument for biodiversity and genetic variation, which huge agribusinesses have bred out of most of what they grow and we eat and use. (And remember?—preserving the huge variety of nature's gene pool is one of your big rationales when politically correct nonguerrilla gardeners get on your case.) Moringas grow all through tropical climates like weeds, and developing nations know all about the tree and its magical properties, but have to be convinced to keep on using them rather than the chemical substitutes we send, trying to be helpful (or trying to make money).

The moringa's seeds have coagulating properties, and they can be eaten like peanuts or fried. The immature green seedpods are cooked like string beans and are very nutritious. In indigenous areas, moringa seeds are used to clean dirty water. They're ground up, tied in a piece of cloth, and stirred around in a pot

of water—chemicals in the seeds bind with dirt particles in water, which then form large globules of solids, and the clear water is poured off. The seed oil is used in cooking, as lamp oil, and because it won't spoil it's used as a preservative and even as a lubricant for machinery. The moringa leaves are steamed like spinach, and they're high in vitamins A, B, and C, as well as calcium, iron, and protein. The leaves also serve as natural Brillo. Moringa flowers can be dipped in batter and fried, and they're high in potassium and calcium. The wood makes a blue dye. The seeds and roots also contain an antibiotic. According to what I've read, it controls glucose in diabetics and prevents beri beri, rickets, and scurvy. It reduces swelling, lowers blood pressure, heals ulcers, and is a natural calmant. It also serves as animal fodder and fertilizer. I can't say that I know how moringas serve all of these purposes, but apparently the moringa is quite an astonishing tree. What else could you possibly ask for?

To keep this wondrous tree growing and to preserve all of the above qualities before they're bred out (for instance, if an industrial tree farm wants to grow moringa only for its oil and finds that genetically eliminating its medicinal uses makes the seeds produce more), everyone should start growing one. Unless you can acquire some cuttings on your travels to points tropical—including Florida, where they're called horseradish trees, you'll have to buy some seeds, and you can get them from Jim Johnson in Mississippi: Seedman.com. He says that moringas handily conform to the size and shape of whatever container they're planted in, and they make nice bonsais. And if you live where it's warm enough, you can plant your baby tree outside, where it can grow fifteen feet a year. Because it has a giant taproot, it can survive in horrible soil and desertlike conditions. Truly a magical gift from Mother Nature.

So come on, do your part.

palm

I've been digging up baby fan palms for years (palm leaves either look like fans or big droopy feathers). One particularly good harvesting spot is in front of the local Blockbuster, so I can get a palm and rent a movie at the same time.

It's pretty easy to grow an indoor palm—you've seen them in those huge planting beds in office buildings and malls, and maybe there's a dusty one growing next to the TV in your boyfriend's apartment (if it's not fake). If someone can identify one for you, a kentia is a great houseplant because it survives in indoor light and grows slowly—although outdoors it can get huge. There are palms that never get to be more than a few inches high, if you're going to make an indoor tropical-cum-cactus garden. And there are palms that tolerate both extreme heat and cold, so if you do a little research, you might become famous for having the only palm garden in Pittsburgh or Montreal, if that's what you'd like to be famous for.

The easiest way to start a palm is from a plantlet (an offset), which you can dig up the next time you go to your favorite Caribbean island or Miami Beach (if you have to make do with a regular indoor tropical palm). They grow at the base of the mother (not all varieties) and are tough to dig up, so put a sharp knife in your suitcase.

If you have time, scrape away the earth to expose the roots and preserve as many of them as you can along with the plant. Keep the plantlet moist in a plastic bag until you get home, then dip the roots in a fungicide and plant it in sand, peat, and grit in a protected, humid area. Of course, if it's the dead of winter where you live, keep it on a sunny windowsill.

Some plantlets have no roots, still getting their nourishment from their mother, like unborn babies. In this case, you can stimulate root growth by cutting a small notch at the base of the plantlet, dusting it with fungicide, and then planting as suggested, keeping it well watered. Cut off all but one leaf, too, to conserve moisture and so that all of the energy can go to making roots. When you are ready to transfer the babies to their more permanent pots, dust the surfaces of the hole you've dug with dolomite to provide magnesium for the roots, which palms really soak up.

Do you remember growing a sickly little plant from a coconut when you were in grade school? Well you can try it now, with a coconut from that same winter vacation (not one you buy at the market). Half-bury it in a deep pot because it will make a long taproot, and just leave it there. The coconut husk will eventually disintegrate, making nutrients for the plant. Don't plant it outdoors (even if your climate allows it) for a few years at least, to keep bugs and other bad things at bay. Whether or not you live in a warm climate, though, palms make terrific long-term potted plants—and you can put them outside in warmer weather—just be sure that they don't get too much sun.

ET CETERA

This could be a much larger category, but you get the idea—you can try growing anything. Just look back at the previous chapter, Capture and Care of Prisoners, to figure out how to propagate or get a big enough sample to try a few different ways, and you're off and running.

spanish moss

Well, it can't get any easier than this. Just climb a tree where some Spanish moss grows, cut off some twelve-inch long strands, climb down, climb up your own tree, and hang your strands over its branches. Of course, you have to live in the right climate, like the Deep South. Or, I don't know, maybe it would work in your bathroom? Hanging over the shower curtain rod?

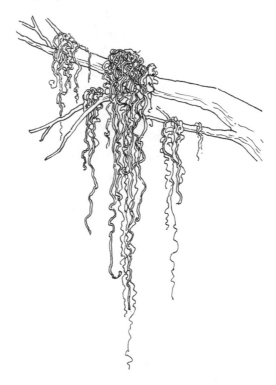

pineapple

Pineapples fall into that category of First Plants—like coconuts and potatoes and avocado seeds. Planting a pineapple top should have been one of your first gardening experiments, the thing that grew in the kindergarten science corner, along with a couple of bugs and maybe a turtle, or maybe your mother showed you how to start one on the kitchen windowsill.

If your supermarket leaves the tuft of thick, sharp foliage on top of its pineapples, you can slice it off, leaving about a half inch of the fruit. Then scoop this out, dip in fungicide, and let the plant dry for a few days. Put the plant in a pot in planting medium, keep it at room temperature, and it should be rooted in a couple of weeks.

Once your pineapple is growing, it should develop shoots. You should break these off, cut cleanly (they won't have roots), break off the lower leaves that would have gone underground, and plant to produce some more pineapples.

CHAPTER FIVE

CAMP MAINTENANCE

Once you've taken your captives and provided some basic conditioning, you'll want them to settle in comfortably. In this chapter, I'll discuss the various aspects of completing your mission.

MOVING YOUR PLANTS TO THE ADULT WING

Here's some information on guerrilla-style ways to prepare your sprouted, rooted plantlet for its next home—its own pot, where you can continue to coddle it in a protected environment, or right into the ground.

For the latter, you will need to understand soil enhancements. Although not totally accurate, I think of mulch, compost, and soil this way: the first becomes the second, which finally becomes the last.

mulch

Mulch is whatever substance you put around plants:

- To keep moisture in the soil
- To keep weeds from growing
- To regulate the temperature of the earth
- To protect those that can take winter but just barely
- To heat the earth to help germination
- To keep the earth cool in blistering weather
- To prevent a strong rain from compacting your carefully cultivated soil, causing it to harden into impermeability when it dries out
- To prevent hard rain from splashing disease-bearing dirt on your plants
- To decompose and become enriched soil

If you just let the dead matter under your plants and trees stay where it falls, however, you have mulch—it happens naturally. Bare earth is not a sign of a tidy garden—it's ugly, it's not natural and it's not healthy for what grows there. Pine needles and hard leaves, like evergreen magnolia, oak, and holly, take a long time to decompose, but they do, eventually. Mulch holds water so that it can seep into the ground in sips—not in one big gulp—drawing oxygen with it, which roots need.

If you happen to live where they grow rice, cotton, or hay, maybe you can get their byproducts—free if possible. Rice hulls, cotton gin waste, dried straw, and hay make great organic mulches.

If you're just starting your garden, though, and haven't got a source of natural mulch, you can use some alternatives: chipped bark from tree removal services as they're working away in your neighborhood (shredded is better and decomposes faster—if you can find it). You can also try coconut husks (also hard to find), and newspaper (shredded if possible, otherwise in layers with a bit of soil sprinkled on top to hold it down). Don't use newspaper with colored print. Just cover it with dirt. And if you really want to get fancy, you can make a slurry, a kind of papier-mâché paste, of your Sunday *Times,* by mixing it with water in a big trash can. Just be sure to cultivate it in with the existing soil—otherwise its density will prevent roots from spreading.

You can also use slit-open black garbage bags (weighted down with rocks), especially if you're in a cold climate. Poke holes in the bags where your seeds or cuttings are planted, so they can grow through (of course, we all know that plastic doesn't decompose, so you'll have to pull this up eventually). You can even lay down old carpeting on an area where you're not going to plant anything immediately. It will protect against weeds and rain runoff.

> **A NON-GUERRILLA TIP**
>
> The one expensive garden tool I have is a vacuum-mulcher. It sucks up dead organic matter from the ground and shreds it so it reduces to about 10 percent of its original mass. I bought a few really long extension cords because you have to plug it in, and I found out that you absolutely must wet down the canvas bag your leaves and so forth collect in, or you will start choking on the dust it accidentally sucks up. It is fabulous for making fast-decomposing mulch that you can then just deposit back where you got it from.

compost

Compost is the caviar of gardening—it's what you mix into soil to enrich it, and it's pure organic matter. You can now buy it, but serious gardeners do it themselves. They toss onto a pile all vegetable matter, including the rotting vegetables from the fridge, grass clippings if they insist on having a lawn, autumn leaves (no more nostalgic burning-leaf-on-the-autumn-air smell), their rabbit's droppings, and so on, chopped up as finely as is practical. The stuff really needs to be chopped up, so no logs, not even twigs, are allowed. They keep it moist and turn it over every once in

a while until they get a rich, dark brown, *odorless,* crumbly substance that looks like the best dirt on earth. If you really want to
get into it, you can buy a composter that you rotate like a bingo
number spinner or build one of wood or fencing, but really, you
need only a pile. Ideally it should be about three by three by three
feet (a cubic yard) to create enough heat, retain enough moisture, and provide enough air circulation (the three ingredients of
successful composting) to decompose what's in it. (But I once had
a taxi driver in New York who told me his pile—out in Queens—
was about twenty by twenty by ten feet high! He also told me
he was broke, and I told him there were plenty of rich, lonely
women in New York who might fix that situation, but he wasn't
too hopeful. You don't have to be as ambitious as he was, but don't
try anything smaller than a cubic yard.) And you don't need to
buy compost chemicals, either—at the most you can add a bit of
manure to speed the process—sprinkle it on every time you add
a six-inch layer of leaves, or whatever. Keep building your pile
until it's the height it should be, then don't add anymore—you
don't want new material added to what's been cooking for a
while. Hard leaves and pine needles take about twice as long as
other material to decompose. The three things to avoid are: adding
weeds that have already gone to seed, unless you want to have a
weed garden; adding diseased plants; and adding waste from meat-
eating animals. There are tons of books on composting if you
want to get serious about it.

soil

Soil is simply what's in the ground naturally. In some places it's a
lot richer and more inviting to plant life than in others. In fact,
there's really no ideal soil for everything that grows. Some stuff is
anathema, though: soil that's been over-worked, doesn't drain, is
mostly rock, that kind of thing. And some is unique—like sand—
or tundra. If you have just ordinary dirt, though—sort of light

brown when dry, you'll be okay with a bit of help, what's called soil amendment. This requires cultivating—churning the soil up with a shovel and elbow grease (my garden designer friend had a bulldozer come into her backyard and I swear it went down three feet). Then you add topsoil, which, if you're lucky, you can get from someone who has great topsoil naturally. Finally, you'll want to add fertilizer. If you know anyone who keeps chickens or horses or sheep, give him a call.

soil additives

To make your earth more hospitable, try one or more easy soil additives.

GREEN MANURE

Green manures are for the really lazy guerrilla gardener. Just fold in leaves, weeds (be absolutely sure they don't have seeds yet), grass clippings, clover, and the like, and leave it on top of the soil—or just let dead foliage stay where it falls—what do you think mulch is? Offer to take away your neighbor's for free—you might gain an ally.

Note: pine needles are very acidic and make great mulch for alkaline soil like mine. I do start skimming off the top layer when they get more than six inches deep, otherwise nothing can grow through them, and they will also start keeping rain from getting into the ground (as opposed to keeping it there).

ANIMAL MANURE

Use manure from non-meat-eating animals only, not your cat or dog or snake or pot-bellied pig. Rabbit droppings are great, and, of course, if you happen to have a horse or live near a chicken farm or. . . . You have to let chicken manure age first, otherwise it will burn delicate roots. (I have no idea how to explain this, but . . . we have two, big, meat-eating dogs; they have a cement run out back, and their doo-doo gets scooped up and put in a trashcan with a sprinkling of lime. Why? Because my mother-in-law used to do this when she lived in a many-terraced apartment in a sixteenth-century building in Rome—the top terrace was saved for Binky, the nasty dachshund who loved to bite Big Guy whenever we visited. Anyway, it was the Big Guy's order at our house, so I did it. I couldn't bear to ask the gardener to empty out this huge container of poop when it got full, so I dug a hole down the hill a bit, and holding my breath, started shoveling the stuff in. When I finally gasped for air, I found out that there was no odor whatsoever. I have no idea what happened, because after all manure is manure. And nothing died. Go figure.)

On the subject of manure: at a local boarding-school, horseback riding was mandatory. I started wondering about what they did with all of that manure, and I wrote to them with some suggestions (after all, schools are always looking for money, right?). I never heard back from them: either they thought I was nuts or they had already been selling it for years.

SAWDUST

If you happen to have a buddy who's an amateur carpenter or hobbyist with a chainsaw in his garage, chances are you'll be able to get some free sawdust. Just be sure to ask if he's working with treated wood because the chemicals aren't good for plant life, especially around things you might be putting on the dinner table. And it's not a good idea to use new sawdust, because it will draw nitrogen out of the soil. Better to let it age a year or so.

SEAWEED

Seaweed's organic. Keep in mind when you're collecting it that people have gotten pretty sensitive about the ecology of beaches, but if you find an inlet with huge, smelly, fly-swarming piles of it, everyone will be happy to see it go. Rinse out the salt first.

COFFEE GROUNDS
Go to your local Starbucks.

potted plants

If you have to garden indoors or move your pots indoors for the winter (or if you just like to plant in pots), there are several essential care requirements. I learned the fundamentals after seeing some of my precious babies turn yellow and sparse at the least, or even die.

The most important item on my list is watering properly. Plants in pots are much, much more sensitive to overwatering or drying out than plants in the ground, which can disperse water or call on reserves of moisture deep down.

I've watered plants heavily, watched the leaves wilt, felt the earth, knew it was wet, shrugged, watered again, and killed the plant. The water drove out the air the plant needs as much as we do to live—it drowned. And constantly wet soil can create an environment that fungi like, which will cause root rot, which will also kill a plant. Be sure your pots have good drainage—you can put a bit of screening over the drain hole, then put a layer of stones or broken crockery on top of that so that water can drain down.

Of course, under-watering is also a problem. I've been known to go on a three-day trip leaving my potted beauties behind in 100-degree-plus weather (Big Guy is definitely not a gardener—turning on the sprinklers is a big deal when I'm gone), and return to at least one dead twenty-year-old plant. I've come to expect it now, although the last time, just a couple of weeks ago, he actually hand-watered the pots (one old scented geranium still died—I guess he didn't see it).

Then you have to fertilize, amend, and even change the earth in pots. Fertilize regularly, because watering eventually leaches the nutrients out of the soil—especially water from your hose. In contrast, I've seen potted plants get a new lease on life after a heavy rain. You can also change the top couple of inches of soil every year, but best of all is to change all of the earth in pots every year or so. Amend the soil with compost and cut back the roots of the plant before you put it back—or put it in a bigger pot.

Another concern with potted plants is that they can become root-bound, that is, the roots have gotten too big for the container. This can cause the leaves to wilt. To remedy the situation, you have to unpot the plant, tease the roots free a bit, and cut them back by half. Or you can replant in a much bigger pot after you've untangled the roots some.

transplanting

If you want to transplant something you've grown from one place to another in your garden, the best time to do it is when it's dormant (provided that the ground isn't frozen). You can also transplant in the spring, but move deciduous plants before they've started budding. A rule of thumb for taking along enough roots with your plant: for every inch of trunk or stem diameter, you need a twelve-inch rootball. Transplanting in hot weather isn't a good idea—the plant is actively growing and disturbing it and severing roots will shock it and stop the growth or even kill it.

VOLUNTEERS, SPORTS AND HEROES

I didn't make up these names—they're genuine garden phenomena. And they can be very useful to a guerrilla gardener.

volunteers

Volunteers are plants that suddenly appear in a garden—either from the self-seeding of a mother plant or from underground rooting. I guess you could say they're the halfway point between a cultivated plant and a weed, and indeed some volunteers grow so voraciously that fussy gardeners think they are weeds and pull them out. But I say, Why do that when nature is doing all your work for you? I got a baby lemon tree through volunteer underground layering by my orange tree—obviously the root stock was a lemon. And every summer baby crape myrtles pop up under their mothers. When you see fields of poppies or daylilies or wild-flowers—well, these are all volunteers, and I would never think of them as weeds.

> **FROM POT TO PLOT**
>
> It's okay to plant a potted plant in the ground any time (weather permitting, of course). This isn't transplanting, because you'll be moving all the earth the plant has grown in along with the plant. You're not disturbing any roots.

A friend of mine built a house right on the sand in Venice Beach, California. The plots are very narrow, and he wanted immediate privacy from his neighbors and passersby on the ocean-front walk not ten feet from the house. So his landscaper brought in an entire ready-made barrier of giant bamboo, bushes with huge leaves, and low palms with fans three feet across. You wouldn't know there was a house there (he gets his view of the ocean and the tan hardbodies in bikinis from the second and third floors of the house).

Verbena is an eager volunteer and can make hundreds of seedlings if you're lucky. If you spot some that's acquirable, get some cuttings, or if you can, divide off a clump with roots. Take greenwood cuttings from nonflowering growth. If you live in a cold climate, make an effort to protect your plantlets—keep them indoors and where they'll get some sun until spring. If you've retrieved a rooted clump, just plant it.

Geranium is also an enthusiastic spreader, and it does so by seeding itself. Another good one is lady's mantle, which is best to propagate via rooted clumps. Ornamental grasses spread like mad, and you should start with a rooted clump, a large one if possible, which you can then divide in the privacy of your own yard and plant. There's a blueberry vine that goes bananas, and it grows best from hardwood cuttings, planted in a frost-free place. It's deciduous, and the leaves and berries are brilliantly colored.

Volunteers are usually much healthier and grow much faster than plants you buy.

sports

Sports are a rare phenomenon, but they do happen, and if one pops up in your garden, it could be like winning the lottery. What occurs is this: all of a sudden a plant starts growing differently— a different color, a different growth pattern, like a bush suddenly becoming a climber. To win the lottery, you have to realize that you've fathered a sport. You must show it to the experts, who in turn must grow it for many years to make sure it doesn't metamorphose back to its old self. Then, if it stays true to its new form, a new plant has been born. It can then be propagated and sold by nurseries all over the world, with your name on the tag—and hopefully paying royalties to you!

heroes

Heroes are trees that either by their size or perfect shape define a landscape. They're also called specimen trees, and people with lots of money to spend or designers of major public or commercial landscapes can afford to buy them—for you don't grow them from a little cutting or rootlet. They're found in old neighborhoods, on the grounds of old estates, and in forests. Moving them is difficult and sometimes not successful.

I remember a beautiful mature ficus tree, about twenty feet in diameter (the tree, not the trunk), planted by the guarded entrance to a gated community years ago. Sadly, it died within six months. The landscaper didn't try again—he just planted ground cover where it had been. I could have told him that the soil in that particular place is a nightmare and only by amending it to great depth would the tree have made it.

If you must acquire a hero, your first order of business is to make sure that its climate and earth are very similar to yours—remember even if it gets cold in Chicago and in New Jersey, they each have a different kind of cold. And the earth at my son's house—he lives a few miles away—is totally different from mine. If your earth is the same as the tree's, you don't have to amend it—just fertilize a bit—and replace the same earth that you dug out to make room for the rootball.

I'd say that if your favorite great aunt dies and leaves her little bungalow to you, and if in the backyard a beautiful seventy-five-year-old red maple is still going strong, and you're going to put the house on the market anyway, go for it—offer it to an upscale nursery or a garden designer and make some bucks.

BORDER PATROL

Of course, I have nothing personal against our animal friends, and in fact, rather like them. They can, however, do a mean business on your hard-earned loot. So to keep your garden intact, you'll want to deter animals and insects while doing both your plants and the invaders the least amount of harm.

animal repellents

Poisonous, sticky plants, or those with an unpleasant texture or nasty taste, will keep deer and other animals away, but be warned— they'll eat anything if they or the winter has finished off their favorite food source. Thorny plants, such as the Natal plum I have in my yard, will also do a nice job of deterring uninvited guests.

Because they emit the odor of humans, hair trimmings are effective against wild animals (but you have to be the family barber, as I am, unless you have the nerve to ask a salon, preferably your own). Put them in the foot end of a stocking and hang at head level against deer and raccoons, lower for rabbits. Hanging mirrors and silvery tape sometimes keep deer and other larger animals away.

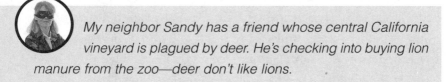

My neighbor Sandy has a friend whose central California vineyard is plagued by deer. He's checking into buying lion manure from the zoo—deer don't like lions.

Not a guerrilla method (i.e., you have to buy them), but I saw in a seed catalogue once that the bulbs of crown imperial tulips, in addition to being huge, have a scent that repels gophers and moles.

Most nonchemical, commercial products made to protect your garden against wild animals and insects are simply a mixture of common ingredients you can make in your own kitchen for a lot less money. Use garlic, rotten eggs, hot pepper flakes, vinegar, and dish soap, pureed in the blender, then diluted with water. Easy as pie, although I sure wouldn't want to taste it. It helps to add an anti-transpirant spray, which is very sticky and will keep the stuff from washing off leaves. If you can find it in a restaurant supply or discount canned goods store, you might buy a huge bottle of hot sauce, and just try that—buying it from a pest-control firm can cost more than $100 for a gallon. If you're worried about harming birds, don't—it doesn't bother them at all, for some reason. You can also try rotten eggs by themselves, which is less offensive than having to mix them in your blender, because you can just crack them open out in the fresh air and run.

Try the above mixture (or a reasonable facsimile) to deter rabbits from gnawing around the soil line of trees and bushes. Or tear up an old sheet (so you have six-foot-long strips), dip the strips into the repulsive (but nonpoisonous) mix, and wrap them around the trunk. If skunks or squirrels are the problem, try using rags soaked in ammonia.

You can also try elephant garlic rubbed directly on your tree trunks (two or three feet above ground level for deer, lower for rabbits). As an alternative, try planting a bed of garlic or chives, which you can then mow. The odor should keep animals (as well as many bugs) away.

> **FREEDOM FROM FELINES**
>
> It's not generally known that cats really don't like the smell of citrus. To keep cats off your trees, rub the trunks with some citrus fruit.

Perhaps the ultimate in guerrilla gardening is to use human urine. I haven't tried it. I guess I could strew my baby granddaughter's very wet diapers around, or offer to take them off the hands of a childcare center, but I think I'd ultimately prefer the pesky animals—and who knows—maybe animals can tell that it's harmless baby pee. A rather pricey option (think about harvesting it!) is to buy coyote, fox, wolf, cougar, or bobcat pee to frighten off deer and other animals. I once bought a tiny, expensive bottle of cougar pee concentrate for my sister, whose garden in Sag Harbor gets ravaged every week by flower-loving deer. I don't think she ever used it—she just buys new plants every weekend.

insect repellent

For bugs that injure and kill plants, you can plant flowers that attract beneficial insects—the ones who eat the bad guys. Ladybugs and praying mantises are well-known bad bug eaters and they're both pretty attractive as insects go. Try rosemary, fennel, nasturtium, yarrow, angelica, alyssum, anise, and any yellow flowers— marigold, a deep orangish-yellow, is a famous repellent. There's also a flower called ebony shoofly with gorgeous blue flowers and purple stems, whose leaves contain alkaloids that bugs don't like.

A simple blast of the hose works on aphids, but only if they haven't established a beachhead. Then you have to keep at it for a few days to really discourage them. I've been doing it to my son's emerging rosebuds, and it definitely works. If aphids have really gotten a hold, use soapy water.

For whiteflies, which when they've really settled in make furry beards underneath leaves, an oscillating sprinkler works best. I use a hose with a nozzle that delivers a really strong stream on my son's hibiscus bushes, which are plagued by whiteflies. You have to do it every other day until they finally give up and set up house at your neighbor's. (I also use a hard spray on my pine trees to wash off dust and smog and dead needles. The spray reaches up about twenty feet, and sometimes I get on my roof to do it, which adds another ten feet. I clean many of my other trees this way, too—and it nourishes them.)

Most of us know that some birds eat an extraordinary amount of bugs every day. You can make your own yard hospitable to birds by giving them somewhere to live and eat. Of course, different birds live in different climates, so you'll have to check out their habitats. For clearing your yard of insects, try to attract purple martins. You don't have to buy a fancy house for a colony of them, which is the way they like to live; you can make entrance holes in gourds (which you can grow!) and hang several of them together. Orioles love orange nectar, so you can make a feeder for

The most amazing bird attack I ever saw was in a beautiful Italian hill town at dusk. Birds were swarming about seventy-five feet overhead, attacking huge beetles, which then fell to the ground with a big clatter, where the birds alighted to eat them. Ugh.

them. You can cobble together an owl house, although they have been known around my yard to eat baby birds and squirrels, so I myself wouldn't welcome them—I've actually tried using a slingshot on them, which they completely ignored. Hummingbirds of course love nectar, which you provide by planting flowers; but you can also put out a dish of nectar you can make in your kitchen, with water, red food coloring, and sugar. Change it every day in hot weather because bacteria will form.

A low retaining wall of unmortared pieces of what once was a cemented driveway.

And then there are bats, which I am irrationally afraid of (although when not flying, and up close, they have adorable little faces). In addition to being big bug eaters, they're a species that needs protection so you'd be doing double duty by making a house for them. Bats live in colonies, so unfortunately you really can't house just a few. If you do decide to go this route, note that bats like to enter their dwelling from underneath, and your bat cave will need to be accessible at the bottom.

SURPLUS

If you're at all like me, you've always got at least one eye open for usable junk. On a recent trip to New York, I saw a great armchair and a new futon frame put out on the sidewalk for the trash man. So the possibilities still exist even there, where I indulged in this method of home decorating many years ago, and which has been chic for a long time, too. Décor for your garden can be more downscale than what you'd put in your house.

Here are some ideas for your garden, culled from my own forays.

We had an apartment in Milan once with a huge wrap-around terrace, and because we had no money, it was fortunate that in Europe they didn't know yet that used furniture—as opposed to that hideous eighteenth-century shiny curvy Louis bronze doré—was really cool. So we got great stuff for nothing. We needed furniture for the terrace, and I saw some fairly uninteresting bricks at a demolition site and borrowed them, a few a day, until I had enough. I made a table out of them, about thirty inches square, I think, and eighteen inches high. I was really happy I hadn't spent much money on stuff there because as it turned out we left six months after we arrived.

rocks and other stuff like rocks

Obviously, rocks are very easy to gather, and why pay for them? Use them decoratively, to shore up a small hill, or to make steps or a wall (mortared or without). Be sure you're not taking stones from a protected area, like a national park or wildlife preserve. Often those beautiful rounded river rocks are in a DMZ too.

In irregular, broken pieces, excavated cement is often put out on the curb for all takers. It makes nice mortarless walls, great stepping stones, or even a driveway (plant grass or a fragrant herb like lemon thyme in between pieces). You can also stack it to make risers for steps, and half-buried on a small hill it's a good earth retainer. Or you can even make a seat with a back against a hill—just secure the back piece with some cement. If you don't like the gray color, you can stain it with iron sulfate, which turns it a beautiful rust.

Beach pebbles can make a nice garden path, and you can use them in glass flower vases. Gather coarse sand for mixing into the soil for succulents and cactus, and even roses (for which you have to use river sand, because beach sand's salt will kill your plants). I also replenish the sand between the bricks, which are not mortared, on my terrace (do not use sandy soil—I tried this two years ago and am still trying to hose and sweep out the pebbles).

> **THE VALUE OF "HEIRLOOM" GARDENING TOOLS**
>
> If you're cleaning out your grandmother's garage and come across some old garden tools, hang onto them. Watering cans, cast iron sprinklers, even old bug sprayers can be worth a fortune. So either make an outdoor shelf to display them or sell them on the 'Net and make money.

wood "waste"

Some people around here cut up their Christmas trees and leave the logs for the recycling truck. I take them, age them for a year,

**PLANT CONTAINERS
ON THE CHEAP**

Look for discarded plant containers behind nurseries, at curbsides, waiting for the trash collector, and around unoccupied or abandoned buildings. You probably have some in the basement, so don't overlook your own home. If you show up at yard sales or swap meets at the end of the day, you can often get pots and the like for next to nothing.

and use them. Watch also for trees that have fallen in storms, and if the tree removal people are just going to put everything in the chipper, ask if you can't have some wood before they do.

I think old wood kitchen chairs, which you can still get cheap at yard sales and thrift shops, look great in the garden—either painted, peeling, or stripped. And it's best when none of them match. A friend of mine has about twenty of them, all done in gold paint.

As to other furniture, check out your own attic. You can put an old

An example of a possible source for homemade walls and steps.

This is my very favorite—I think it was a collaborative effort by Big Guy and me, when we moved in here so long ago. He wanted an outdoor table that you could just hose off, so there would be no dishes to wash (he's a guy, right?). I had always loved those huge wooden spools that industrial cable is wound on—at least they used to be wood. They were about six feet in diameter, and they looked just like tables. I somehow found one, hauled it home, and got it up onto our terrace. I dug around in my treasures and found some great old dishes—Coal Miner's Union of West Virginia, some Colorado jubilee celebration, stuff like that, and rounded up other oddities like old keys (we all have a drawer full of them), shells, and a Cunard Lines ashtray. I also scrounged some tinny silverware, and we made a cement top on the table and laid in all of the above, eight place settings, with our son's eight-year-old palm print for good luck. Hosing off went by the boards, of course (rotting smoked salmon in the bushes?), but I did buy some glass dishes so you could see the ones underneath. We had some great drunken Easter brunches out there, before the cement developed some serious faults (this being earthquake country) and we had to dismantle everything—but I saved the dishes (and the kid's handprint) for a future venture.

chest of drawers in a corner, leave the drawers open haphazardly or in tiers, line them with plastic garbage bags, and garden away. A friend gave me a lovely, nineteenth-century wicker table when she moved about twenty years ago. It wasn't in great shape then, and it's barely hanging on now, but it's partially hidden by a very prolific tiny-leafed potted ivy that another friend left me when she moved. I love the look—it's right on the way to my front door (it is protected somewhat by a four-foot roof overhang and a wall of the house).

lights

Lights are a pain in the garden—you either have to have wiring, or use candles, which in fire-prone country is not an option, really. I leave on indoor lights near my terrace and deck, so the light can flow out, and I have some really long extension cords and put lamps out there. From some remodeling job, I inherited some work lights that clip onto wherever you need them. I've climbed into our pine tree and stuck them up there, shining upward, to cast an ambient glow below. Then there are always those little white Christmas lights, which around where I live have begun to stay up all year on some decks and porches. I've even seen funny old chandeliers wired and hanging from trees. If you're at all mechanical, you can even install neon or laser lights in your garden—just don't overdo it or you'll look like you're running a theme park.

In France a secretive group, and maybe individual copycats, have been stealing those paragons of bad taste, garden gnomes (you'd think the French would scorn such things). This is a really serious thing—homeowners love these Disney rip-offs as though they were their own children, taking them in at night, bathing them, putting them to bed. But it doesn't seem like the thieves are railing against bad taste. They "kidnap" these Dopeys and Snoopys and liberate them in their "natural" environment, the forest. There's even been a university conference on the phenomenon, and, of course, a Web site (www.menj.com).

root cellar

A root cellar is out if you live in the tropics, but it should be okay as long as you get some really cool nights and choose a shady site. What is it? A twenty-first-century version of your grandmother's unheated, dirt–floor cellar, where out-of-season vegetables and fruits—which we can now, of course, get year-round—were stored, along with the home-canned peaches and the hanging salamis. You might like to make one of these if you don't have a cellar. You might also want to think about a root cellar if you have an overabundant crop of delicious home-grown fruits or vegetables and your friends now run for cover when they see you approaching with armfuls of sweet potatoes.

Use an old fridge, with, of course, the door-locking machinery removed, or some of those big Styrofoam shipping cartons (I get them when I order something like a Smithfield ham or special Italian New Year's Eve sausages from New York). Even try an old Styrofoam picnic cooler, but be sure to surround it with strong chicken wire to keep out hungry burrowing animals. Bury your container up to the lid. Don't wash the vegetables and fruits to be stored, but wrap them individually in newspaper to hold in moisture. Never store fruits next to vegetables as the fruit may exude gases that will rot the veggies. And never use plastic bags or containers not made expressly for food because they can contain dangerous chemicals. This is a fairly complicated process, and not everything can be stored successfully, so read up on it before you start.

A friend did a fabulous major birthday party (with a zero in the number, okay?) for another friend and me out in the Hamptons a while ago. She has a major Kilim rug collection, so she put about twenty of them out on the grass under one very long table, and it looked absolutely great. If you have any once-good rugs that really can't make it in the house anymore (chewed up by the dog or totally wrecked by a housekeeper who insists on using the vacuum's motorized rotor brush) and you have a nice, flat, partially shaded area—a terrace or even dirt—give it a try. It's also a good idea for a sisal rug that's absorbed too many red wine stains— sort of an intermediate stop before the garbage can.

I have three great canopies—well, I guess they became canopies—that I use over our deck once in a while. One is sheer natural muslin, which in my more energetic youth I stitched up on my sewing machine to make an exotic tent for my apartment bedroom's sixties-era cottage cheese ceiling. It's got to be about forty by forty feet, and I tacked it up in great festoons. It worked, then I didn't use it again for years. One Fourth of July, we had a party to watch the fireworks over the city and I put it up. I draped it over pine branches, tacked it to the roof and over the magnolia, and it looked great. When I use it, I just make sure to keep the votive candles far away.

other matériel

A garden provides a great spot for all sorts of items that would otherwise be tossed out. Some of my favorite reusable refuse includes:

- Old shoes—if they're leather or canvas they'll even compost out in a few years
- An old wheelbarrow (not for growing edibles unless you're certain of what's been in it)
- Broken crockery from your kitchen, like a teapot that's lost its spout, for decorative pots (in which to put planting pots with drainage holes)
- Chipped dishes for pot liners
- Wooden crates—you can partially bury them and have an instant planting bed with protection against burrowing animals
- Wicker baskets, lined with plastic
- Battered toys—not plastic, for the sake of aesthetics, unless you're making a Gen-X garden
- Old bathroom appliances—we've all seen bathtubs, sure, but in the depths of blue-collar Maine I spotted an old toilet brimming over with a lush, flowering vine

- An old garbage can cover, for a birdbath. Put some gravel in the bottom, disguise the edges with stones, or set it into some lush foliage that will partially cover it
- An old ladder, to make frames for a little herb garden—wooden is, of course, more aesthetically pleasing than aluminum
- Driftwood
- Mirrors—no, honestly. I was going to trash a thirty-inch square mirror from a remodeled bathroom when Big Guy took it and hid it in dense foliage near the front door—scaring arriving dinner guests who thought they were being jumped by Jack the Ripper in that instant before they realized that they were looking at their own sinister selves

Another canopy is a bright, multicolored, handpatchworked thing I bought in Egypt, I think—I can't remember. It's great for hot summer brunches when the deck doesn't get enough shade. With that one, because it's much heavier, I string rope from our roof to the trunk of a pine tree (about fourteen feet up) and drape the fabric over that, the "done" side down, of course, so diners can see it. I tack the sides (actually nail them) to the roof, and it becomes an instant tent. The third one is a fabulous camouflage-pattern, full-sized parachute (premonition of guerrilla warfare to come?) that I bought in an army surplus store to cover a sofa our dogs used (after we gave up and gave it to them, and bought ourselves a new one). It looked kind of funny, but now you can actually buy these instant slipcovers for your upholstered furniture. Anyway. New dogs, new furniture, and I packed the parachute away until another brunch, another tent. The dappled green light was beautiful and cooling. You can even do this with a king-sized sheet tied at the corners to some long bamboo poles stuck in the ground. Or that old bedspread. Or . . .

CHAPTER SIX

FREE FOOD

The following are some less than ordinary recipes based on captures you might make.

WILD THINGS

You'll have to learn what wild foods look like because you don't want to poison yourself. (One rule of thumb: if something smells like peaches or bitter almonds, or if it's slimy, stay away.) There are lots of books about gathering wild plants to eat. One of my favorites is *Stalking the Wild Asparagus,* which has been on the shelf next to my bed for years. Don't think of gathering wild plants to eat unless you're with an expert or have become an expert yourself.

piñon cakes

Piñon nuts, as they are known in the southwest, are from piñon pines, but check out any unopened pinecones that you come across in your travels. Not all pines produce edible nuts in their cones. You'll have to find out through local lore. Piñon nuts might have a tough shell, in which case you should soak them overnight before cracking with a nutcracker.

These nuts are called pinoli in Italy, where they are used in pasta (my favorite is with broccoli, raisins, anchovies, and tomato sauce—and who could forget pesto), and just plain pine nuts in most other places. I had a huge argument years ago in a supermarket with the produce guy who insisted that piñon nuts were not the same as pinoli. The customer is always right? I thought this guy was going to punch me out, he was so angry, so I left.

   2 cups raw, shelled piñon nuts
   ¾ cup water
       dash of salt
   2 Tbs. olive or vegetable oil

Purée nuts in a blender and mix with water and salt in a medium-sized bowl. Let stand 15 minutes. Heat oil in a skillet and drop batter in by tablespoonfuls and brown on both sides. Eat hot as a vegetable side dish or at room temperature as an hors d'oeuvre. Very rich.

Makes about 25 cakes.

piñon soup

    1 lb. raw, shelled piñon nuts
    ½ tsp. coriander seeds
        dash of salt
        dash of pepper
    2 cups chicken broth
    2 scallions, chopped
    1 tsp. crushed dried mint leaves
    1 qt. milk
    1 cup water

Combine all ingredients in a large saucepan and bring to a boil. Lower heat and simmer, stirring constantly for 30 minutes. Puree in blender, in batches if necessary. Serve hot or cold with toasted, crumbled corn tortilla chips.

Makes 8 servings.

piñon nut gravy

    2 cups raw, shelled piñon nuts
        water to cover
        dash of salt

Chop piñon nuts with a knife or grind in a blender but not too fine. Place nuts in a large saucepan and cover them with water. Boil until oil from the nuts rises to the surface, about 30 minutes. Skim off the oil, boil again, and season with salt.

lamb's quarters salad

Lamb's quarters, also called purslane, are a spinachlike plant (and actually a member of the spinach family), that you can use raw in a salad or cooked. You can also blanch or parboil the leaves and freeze them for later use, and some people even can them. Use tender young plants, less than a foot high.

4 slices bacon
1 medium onion, chopped
¼ cup vinegar
    dash of salt
4 cups tender tops of lamb's quarters, washed and drained

Fry bacon in a skillet until crisp. Remove bacon with a slotted spoon and let drain on paper towels. Sauté the onion in the bacon fat until golden, then add the vinegar and salt. Let mixture simmer for 1 to 2 minutes. Add lamb's quarters and let simmer until just limp. Turn into a serving bowl. Crumble the bacon and sprinkle over top. Serve hot.

Makes 4 servings.

lamb's quarters quiche

    shell for bottom crust of one pie (homemade or commercial)
 4 cups chopped lamb's quarters, washed
 1 Tbs. butter
 ½ cup chopped onion
 ½ tsp. salt
 3 eggs
1¾ cups whole milk
 2 cups grated Swiss cheese

Preheat oven to 450°F. Partially bake pie crust for 6 minutes, remove from oven, and turn oven down to 325°F. Melt butter in a large skillet, add onions and sauté until golden at medium heat. Add lamb's quarters and stir in salt. Cook for 1 minute on low, then remove from heat. In a separate bowl, beat together the eggs and the milk. Add the lamb's quarters and the Swiss cheese to the egg mixture and stir. Pour into pie shell. Bake 45 minutes at 325°F. Let stand 10 minutes before serving.

Makes 8 servings.

wild mustard

Use the young leaves and yellow flowers raw in salads. Or you can cook the most tender shoots. Wash, drain, and cook shoots in a skillet at a simmer for 20 minutes. Add ¼ cup of water occasionally as liquid boils off. Add dash of salt when cooking is complete. Serve with melted butter or vinaigrette dressing.

dandelion greens

If you grew up the way I did, every summer having to pull out the "crabgrass" (does it even exist anymore?), you'll know what a dandelion looks like. In fact, I can never forget what one looks like. After a heavy day of weeding, when I'd close my eyes to go to sleep—I was about fourteen—they'd pop right up. You know the phenomenon. If you, however, don't know what dandelion looks like, search out a plant with longish, lobed leaves and cheerful yellow flowers, or flip through your wild things book. Then yank it out of the ground—you can pretend you're weeding (aren't you?). When you get home, try this recipe.

1 qt. or more dandelion greens
dash of salt
olive oil to taste

Pick and clean at least 1 quart of greens (it boils down like spinach). Rinse it well and steam in a saucepan for 3 minutes. Whatever moisture remains on the greens will be sufficient. No other water is necessary. Serve at room temperature with salt and olive oil.

Makes 2 servings.

boiled acorns

Acorns can be very bitter, so before you use them in cooking, be sure to eliminate the tannins that cause this.

Boil unshelled acorns in water for 15 minutes, then shell and boil them in fresh water for another 15 minutes. Taste and boil again if necessary.

Use for Park Nuts or other recipes.

park nuts

I had to include this one because of its name. It comes from a guy who's called the wild man of Central Park.

3 cups water
¼ cup fresh lemon juice
4 large, peeled garlic cloves, minced
¼ cup plus 2 Tbs. curry powder
1 qt. boiled acorns (page 186)
3 Tbs. olive oil
1 tsp. salt

Preheat oven to 300°F. Boil 2½ cups of water in large saucepan. As it boils, pour remaining ½ cup of water, lemon juice, garlic, and ¼ cup curry powder in the blender. Blend until smooth and add to boiling water along with acorns. Simmer 5 minutes, drain acorns. Mix acorns with olive oil, salt, and 2 tablespoons curry powder in a large roasting dish. Roast for 45 to 90 minutes; remove from oven when acorns have the texture of roasted chestnuts. Test occasionally to make sure acorns aren't becoming hard.

Nancy used to have a catering business and she's a great cook. She passes by a particular lemon tree on her daily walks (I know, because I walk with her) when she's going to make the world's most fabulous (two pounds of butter) lemon layer cake. The tree hangs right over the road, and its owners never seem to harvest it, so Nancy does.

fiddlehead ferns

When baby ferns are just emerging from the ground, they are tightly furled and look like the carved end—where the strings are tuned—of a violin, thus the name. They stay this way for about two weeks, during which time you can gather them (in Alaska and the northeast).

Rinse the ferns, pat them dry, then sauté them in butter at medium heat for ten minutes, or use them raw in salad.

pyracantha jelly

1 qt. red, ripe berries

3 pts. water

¼ cup lemon juice

¾ cup orange juice

1 package of powdered pectin

4½ to 5½ cups sugar

Wash berries and boil in water in large saucepan for 20 minutes. Strain out berries through cheesecloth, or if you'd like a little texture, through a strainer. Return liquid to the saucepan. To 4 cups of berry juice, add lemon juice, orange juice, and pectin. Bring juice mixture to a boil again, and add sugar, stirring for 2 minutes. Pour into sterilized jars and seal. (I don't like my food supersweet; taste the juice as you add sugar to arrive at what your taste buds like.)

CITRUS

lemon leftovers

Juice extra lemons, and freeze the juice in tiny containers, like old spice bottles, for use when you need lemon juice in a recipe but don't have a lemon. (I love to use my juicer, an ancient Kitchen Maid mixer-meat-grinder-juicer which my son's friends admire for its antiquity. I know I must be getting really old, because it was a wedding present—not to my grandmother, but to me.) Anyway.

I've been eyeing a row of fruit-laden citrus trees on my son's block. Oranges, tangerines, lemons, the ground is littered with fallen ones, the lawn is a foot high, no one's home. So the other day I plucked some of each fruit to try out. Delicious. I went back and did a nice harvest, leaving plenty on the trees. Twenty lemons, twenty tangerines, twenty oranges (even though I have a tree of my own, the fruit is still tiny and green).

citrus skins

When you've managed to grow a fruit-bearing tree from your cutting, but the fruit tastes awful (usually a product of that year's climate and rainfall), harvest it anyway. Then peel off the skin, making sure not to get too much of the white inner layer (if you do, scrape it off—it's bitter), and sliver or break the skins into nickel-sized pieces. Brown the skins in a toaster oven—it happens fast, so stay close—and put the toasted skins in a jar, to use later, for Chinese orange-skin or tangerine-skin beef, or lemon pasta, or orange-skin beef stew, for example. Then wait to see what the next year's harvest will be like.

tangerine-skin beef

   3 lb. piece of round steak
     juice of 1 lemon
     dash of tabasco sauce
  10 peeled and halved garlic cloves
  ¼ cup soy sauce
   2 bunches scallions, sliced on the diagonal, discarding tough
     top inch
   1 cup tangerine skins

Freeze the round steak and then semi-defrost it so that it is easy to cut across the grain, diagonally, in thin pieces. Put in a bowl and add lemon juice, tabasco, garlic, and soy sauce and marinate in the fridge for a few hours, turning occasionally. Cook the mixture in a wok at high heat for about 15 seconds, then add the scallions and cook another 15 seconds. Add the tangerine skins and cook for another 10 seconds. Serve with rice. Note: you can also make this dish with orange skins.

Makes 4 servings.

orange-skin beef stew

Make an ordinary beef stew. (I use a pressure cooker; it gets the meat fork-tender.) When stew has almost finished cooking, add pitted Kalamata olives or other Mediterranean olives and toasted orange skins.

FLOWERS

You might not be growing all of them, but surely you can find a couple of blossoms here and there on a morning walk for your dinner party that night. Just don't use flowers from a florist as they might be sprayed with who knows what. And you have to be careful, especially with roses, that you're gathering blooms that haven't been sprayed with insecticide, mold killer, or fertilizer. This stuff can be very dangerous when ingested. Even if you're sure your blooms are organic, rinse them off before you use them in the following recipes. If you aren't sure about a flower, please don't eat it. Some, like oleander, angel's trumpet, and lily of the valley, are poisonous.

Safe flowers include those from herbs (rosemary, thyme, lavender, sage, chive, which all taste like the herbs themselves); roses (like their scent); nasturtiums, geraniums and scented geraniums, marigold (spicy); dianthus, begonia (lemony); carnation (peppery); fuchsia (tart); pansy, calendula (spicy); zucchini (like the vegetable).

rose hip jelly

3½ lbs. wild rose hips, gathered when soft
  3 cups water
  1 cup apple juice
  1 package of powdered pectin
  3 cups sugar

Remove blossom ends of hips, split and discard balls of seeds. Crush hips and put in a large saucepan, add water and apple juice. Simmer, covered, on low heat for 10 minutes. Put mixture in a cloth pastry bag. Tie the top of the bag and hang over a large bowl until all of the liquid has drained through the cloth, making about 4 cups. Mix the pectin with the rose liquid in the saucepan and bring to a hard boil. Add sugar and boil for 1 minute more. Skim the froth from the top and pour into sterilized canning jars and seal.

rose hip tea

Heat oven to 250°F. Place rose hips on a cookie sheet and slowly dry in oven. Store in an airtight container. When you want to make tea, grind enough rose hips to make 1 tablespoon to 1 cup of water. Boil and strain, and add sugar to taste.

rose petal fruit salad

Mix together blueberries and slices of nectarines with a bit of salt. Arrange on plates and sprinkle with raspberry or other fruit vinegar. Toss washed and drained rose petals on top (about 1 rose per serving).

I knew a Middle Eastern hippie in Berkeley once—she looked like a friendly witch—who put rose petals in everything. I especially remember her stuffed chard, which was much tastier than stuffed cabbage. She added cinnamon as well as rose petals to the meat stuffing. It was so good you'd think it was illegal.

rose petal jelly

3 dozen red, very fragrant roses
1 qt. water
4 cups sugar
3 Tbs. fresh lemon juice

Remove petals from the roses by slicing flower across the base, above the white portion at the bottom, which is bitter. Put petals in a large bowl. Boil water and add to petals. Steep for twenty minutes or until all color has leached out of the petals. Strain the liquid into a large shallow skillet. Add the sugar and lemon juice, which will turn the liquid a lovely pink color. Cook at medium heat, stirring the whole time, until the sugar is dissolved and the liquid comes to a rolling boil. Maintain this boil until you reach the "jelly" stage, when two drops will form on the lip of a metal spoon and then flow together to form a film. At this point you can drop in a few tablespoons of rose petals, for looks. Skim any froth off the top and pour into sterilized jars and seal. Note: use this jelly within six months or the color will start to fade.

flower salad

¼ cup orange juice

⅛ cup olive oil

1 Tbs. grated orange peel

salt and pepper, to taste

5 oz. package of washed mixed salad greens

5 oz. package of washed baby spinach

3 cups flowers, like pansies or nasturtiums

1 cup rose petals

Combine juice, olive oil, orange peel, and salt and pepper. Toss with salad greens and baby spinach. Add rinsed and dried whole flowers and rose petals and toss lightly.

Makes 10 servings.

nasturtium pasta

¾ cup marigold petals

4 cups nasturtium blossoms

4 cups nasturtium leaves

1 lb. penne pasta

½ cup lemon juice

½ cup olive oil

⅛ tsp. salt

1 tsp. freshly ground pepper

Rinse, drain, and pat dry petals, blossoms, and leaves. Cook pasta and cool to room temperature. In a large bowl, mix lemon juice, oil, salt, and pepper, and then toss with pasta. Gently mix in flowers and leaves.

Makes 4 servings.

stuffed zucchini flowers

Now you can find these in farmers' markets, but when my mother-in-law made them for lunch twenty-five years ago, I was astounded at the concept and immediately fell in love with the dish. I make them all the time.

½ cup flour
⅛ tsp. pepper
 1 lb. buffalo mozzarella cheese, sliced into 20 pieces
 2 oz. tin anchovy filets
20 zucchini blossoms, rinsed and patted dry
 2 eggs, beaten
½ cup olive oil

Combine flour with pepper and set aside. Put a slice of mozzarella and ⅓ of an anchovy filet in each blossom. Dip blossom in egg and then in flour mixture. Heat olive oil in large frying pan, then gently place blossoms into pan. Cook for 4 minutes, or until browned and mozzarella is melted. Drain on paper towels.

Makes 4 lunch or appetizer servings.

crystallized violets

Sometimes at Easter I make a Russian pudding—it has to be formed in a terra cotta plant pot (new, please) lined with cheesecloth. When you turn it out onto a plate, the pattern of the cheesecloth is visible. I use a big round serving dish and put flowers and crystallized violets around it and on top.

Gather violets—the best specimens you can find. Rinse and pat dry very gently. Beat the white of one egg until soft peaks form—not stiff. Dip each flower in the egg white, shake out very gently, and sprinkle the sugar over all, including the underside. Put on a cookie sheet lined with waxed paper and dry in the fridge for a couple of days. Store in a closed jar in a cool place, layering the flowers with waxed paper.

SUCCULENT SUCCULENTS

yucca sweets

You'll see these dark green, ribbed, plum-sized fruits on the stalks of yucca. I have some out back. Bake in a slow oven several hours until skins can be peeled and the ball of seeds and fiber removed. What's left is a sweet paste you can use in pies or turnovers or shaped into bars and sun-dried or slow-oven-dried to make delicious candy.

My multitalented brother-in-law makes prickly pear jam, along with mulberry jam from his and my sister's own tree, canned peaches from their trees, etc., etc. He can also build any-thing, including computers, which are all over the house.

prickly pear jelly

Prickly pears are the best known of edible cactus, and you can eat both the fruit and the paddles. You can put the latter, peeled and raw, in salads, using baby paddles (*nopalitos*), with prickles and spines burned off. You can eat the fruit plain (delicious), or freeze it or make juice with it. And you can toss a paddle on the barbecue, giving it a smoky flavor, or chop it raw to stuff an omelet.

    3 qts. prickly pears, prickles and spines burned off
    3 cups water
    1 cup lemon juice
    10 to 12 cups sugar
    2 packages of powdered pectin

Put fruit in a large, heavy pot with water. Boil 15 to 20 minutes. Drain fruit and reserve water. Peel, then mash fruit and put the paste back into the water. Cook 5 minutes more. Line a strainer with cheesecloth and strain pulp, letting strained juice stand to settle sediment. Pour off the juice carefully and discard sediment. In a pot, combine 4 cups prickly pear juice, lemon juice, and 3 cups sugar. Bring to a boil, stirring constantly. Add another 2 to 3 cups of sugar, cook and stir until the mixture reaches a full boil, then add 1 package of pectin and continue cooking on high for 15 minutes. Pour in sterilized jars and seal. You should have 4 cups of pear juice left; repeat the process.

A wild roadside stand of prickly pears.

prickly pear salsa

- 4 prickly pear paddles
- 1 onion
- 2 tomatoes
- 2 garlic cloves
- 2 roasted chilies, Anaheim or jalapeño

Use only the brightest green, unwrinkled paddles. Singe off spines and prickles, trim all around the edges of the paddle with a knife, and cut off the thick tough base. Cook paddles in simmering water until done, drain, cool, and chop. Chop onion, tomatoes, garlic, and chilies. Combine all ingredients. To use on tostadas, first put layers of chopped lettuce, cheese, and sliced avocado on the tostada, then top with the salsa.

ODDITIES

loquat jam

In temperate climates you'll find loquats languishing on trees people planted back in the fifties. No one eats them anymore, which is nuts because they're fabulous.

> 4 cups washed, seeded, and coarsely chopped loquats with skins on and juice retained
> 1½ cups sugar
> ¾ cup water
> ½ cup lemon juice

Mix loquats (including juice) with sugar, water, and lemon juice in a large saucepan. Cook until thickened (about 10 minutes), pour into sterilized jars, and seal.

loquat upside-down cake

Peel 10 loquats and remove the seeds. Cook in a large saucepan in 1 cup water for about 15 minutes, until fruit is tender. Add brown sugar to taste. Proceed as you would with any upside-down cake. Or, just eat the stewed loquats as a snack, using white sugar rather than brown.

Makes 5 servings.

loquat salsa

   1 cup peeled, seeded, and chopped loquats
   1 cup peeled and chopped green papaya
   1 tsp. lemon juice
     dash of cayenne pepper
  ¼ cup chopped cilantro
   1 roasted, skinned, and seeded jalapeño chile, finely chopped
   1 tsp. toasted cumin

Combine all ingredients.

Makes about 2½ cups.

fig chutney

   1 medium onion, diced
   1 garlic clove, minced
   1 cup raisins
   1 Tbs. chili powder
   1 cup chopped, crystallized ginger
   2 Tbs. mustard seeds
   1 Tbs. salt
   1 qt. white vinegar
   2 cups lightly packed brown sugar
   8 cups diced, unpeeled figs
   2 mangoes, peeled and diced (optional)

Put onion, garlic, and raisins in a large pot. In a separate bowl, mix together remaining ingredients. Add to saucepan. Simmer on low heat, stirring for 1 hour until deep brown and thick. Pack in sterilized jars and seal.

HEALING HERBS

Herbs have a strong impact on your health, just like prescription drugs. Some herbs are poisonous, so don't go ingesting them willy-nilly—be sure to do your research first.

Of course, if you live in the city or in a cold climate, and want to use personally grown or kidnapped herbs through the winter, you'll have to dry them. I just wash them, gently shake them off, and put them on a paper towel in the kitchen for a few days. My mother grinds up the rosemary and basil she takes from my garden, to bring back east with her, but I prefer it in its natural state. Wash out some spice jars from the supermarket and use them for storage.

chamomile tea

Rinse chamomile leaves and pat dry, then allow to dry completely in the shade. Crumble and store leaves in a cool, dark, dry place. When ready to use, crumble up some to make a tablespoon's worth, put in a cup, and pour boiling water over it.

lavender cookies

Lavender gives an unexpected, grown-up perfume to ordinary cookies.

  12 sprigs fresh, flowering lavender
   2 cups flour
2½ tsp. baking powder
     pinch of salt
  ½ cup (1 stick) butter, room temperature
  ½ cup sugar
  ½ tsp. vanilla extract
   2 Tbs. grated lemon rind
   2 tsp. lemon juice
   1 egg

Preheat oven to 350°F. Strip lavender flowers off stems and chop roughly. Combine flour, baking powder, and salt in a bowl and set aside. In another bowl, cream butter, gradually adding sugar, and beat until light. Add vanilla, lemon rind, and lemon juice. Beat in egg then blend in flour mixture. Mix in lavender flowers gently, by hand. Drop by teaspoonfuls onto greased cookie sheet and bake 10 minutes until golden brown.

Makes 3 dozen cookies.

lavender ice cream

The following is a variation on a theme.

2 cups heavy cream
1/2 cup half-and-half
1/2 cup chopped lavender flowers and leaves
8 egg yolks
1 cup sugar

In a heavy pot, mix cream, half-and-half, and chopped lavender flowers and leaves. Heat slowly, stirring constantly, until warm. Remove from heat and let stand for 30 minutes. In a medium bowl, whisk egg yolks and sugar together for a few minutes, then stream about 1/2 cup of the cream into egg mixture, whisking rapidly (this will keep the egg yolks from curdling when you add them to the warm cream). Return the cream to the flame, adding the egg mixture gradually while stirring constantly. Cook on low heat for about 5 minutes until the mixture begins to thicken. Strain to remove lavender.

> **YUM!**
>
> Big Guy puts a few mint leaves into peas right before they're done cooking, and I use tons of it in iced tea, mushing it up with confectioner's sugar and lemon juice before adding the tea. When I make an Indian dinner, I chop up leaves as a condiment.

Cover mixture and chill in the fridge for about 1 hour. Turn the mixture with a wooden spoon, then put in the freezer, turning every 30 minutes so that it doesn't harden. Serve semisoft and sprinkle lavender blossoms on top of each serving.

Makes 6 servings.

CHAPTER SEVEN

PLUNDER: OTHER USES FOR PLANTS

Here are some ideas for captures that won't become part of your garden, but are nonetheless to be desired for other purposes.

TABLE DECORATIONS

I like the look of "free-style" decor. The following suggestions are nice for holiday time, and when you're giving a dinner party, or just because you like to have something alive in the house. My mother always said you could tell when I was home from college because I'd put flowers all over the house (from our own garden, back then).

eucalyptus

There are a number of eucalyptus trees on my block that have delicate, deep pink flowers at the same time they're bearing those nice little aromatic buttons that hippies used to make necklaces out of.

Raiding the pittisporum.

The branches droop pretty low, and if I park my Land Cruiser up against the curb, I can climb on the roof and get some with a long-handled lopper. So far I haven't had to resort to using a tree pruner—I do think it would be a bit unwieldy, and obvious, to say the least, and not for a quick getaway. Anyway, the branches are quite pretty and look great in a vase or as a table centerpiece, but lying flat so people can see each other.

A recent article in the paper told about a Bureau of Land Management employee who was arrested for "weeding" (getting rid of non-native eucalyptus in the central California still-wild valley where he worked). Sometimes he just pruned back real hard, sometimes he sliced into a tree, which eventually kills it, and sometimes he just chopped them down. He was convicted of vandalism, and his punishment was four days of community service—removing non-native plants from a city creek bed.

magnolia

A huge white blossom is gorgeous on your dinner party table, but it will last just about as long as the dinner. The husband of a friend took to kidnapping magnolia on his evening jogs, but when he got all the lower blossoms he forced his poor young daughter into service (under the guise of good exercise), hoisting her up into the trees for the more inaccessible flowers. By the way, the giant, shiny leaves of magnolia look great mixed with evergreens for the holidays. And the seeds, which are like large, brilliant red shiny lentils, growing from their pinecone-sized pods, are perfect for your little decorating schemes.

bougainvillea

I have a friend who cruises the back alleys of the Beverly Hills flats looking for overhanging bougainvillea—it's fair game. Once you've plucked them, they don't have a long shelf-life, so if you're using them for a centerpiece, you'll want to spend some time in the field on the day of your party.

evergreens

You can usually free all sorts of evergreens, from pines to holly, wherever you live, but you'll probably need a lopper to get anything of usable size. If you're out to get some holly, be sure to wear gloves, as it's really unpleasantly spiky.

pyracantha

These plants or small trees bear huge branches of bright orangish-red berries right around holiday time. They fall off fairly easily, so shake before taking. I put them on my pine door wreath, or on my Christmas or New Year's Eve table, woven in among pine branches.

My stash is three trees on a side street off a main shopping drag, and I've been harvesting from them for years.

Barbara picking pinecones.

pinecones

I save the pinecones that fall off my own trees during the year, and I've been known to screech to a halt when I spot a particularly nice one in the road. I have two enormous pinecones that I found under equally huge pine trees, and I use them every holiday season. I also toss less than perfect pinecones into the fireplace—sometimes they give off a nice aroma.

HINTS FOR HERBS

In addition to food preparation, there are lots of things you can do with herbs. For example, gather a bunch of herbs, let them dry, and put them in the foot of old pantyhose. Let them steep in a nice hot bath and you've got your own aromatherapy. I'd use lavender, rosemary, mint, scented geranium, or rose petals.

The house of a good friend is next to a perpetually empty lot, and when we go to dinner parties there, Big Guy always plucks a few stalks of wild fennel where they grow near the curb, crushes them in his meaty fist, and puts them on the car's dashboard. As they bake in the sun, they impart a nice scent for a day or two—certainly better than those awful "new car scent" hang-ups you buy at the carwash. You can do this with any wild (or untended) herb you come across.

LAVENDER FOR THE LINENS

I break off fading lavender branches, bunch them together, and put them in old pantyhose (the bottom part, with the reinforced toe, is best), tie them with string, and put them in my linen closet. When they need refreshing, I just squeeze them a lot. (By the way, my mother is the pantyhose queen—she's thought up a million ways to use old ones, but that's another book.)

CHAPTER EIGHT

A FAREWELL TO THE TROOPS

More than sixty years ago, my mother planted a pear tree in her mother's garden. When we last looked (she's moved back to the neighborhood after decades in Italy and other places), it was still there. Now that I'm at the age when we get interested in genealogy—as well as gardening—the next time I visit my mother I'm going to ask the current owners if I can take some cuttings from the tree. I'll plant a few for my mother, and take some home. I'd love to be able to give a baby pear tree to my baby granddaughter from her great-great-grandmother.

For all of you fighting the good fight, don't come away from this little tome thinking it's shown you how to function on the fringes of an orderly (?) society or how to save money. Don't believe you've learned how to protect some of our exponentially disappearing wildlife or that you, an ordinary soldier, can. Read this as a manual on how to write your own history. How to make a garden filled with stories . . . your stories . . . your book . . .

NEW TECHNOLOGY FOR THE BATTLEFIELD

I often use the Internet when checking up on something, when I need to learn about a new plant, or when I want to find a source for cuttings. (Yes, you can trade or even get them free— so far there don't seem to be any hackers or cheaters or other nasty types among gardeners on the 'Net.) There are so many gardening Web sites that I couldn't possibly list them all here. (I've come to think of the 'Net as the 3Gs—gardening, golf, and genealogy—the three biggest hobbies in the country. I guess I'll have to write about the other two someday, although I don't know how you do guerrilla genealogy or guerrilla golf.)

There are Web sites for the region you live in—what will do well there, when to plant, and the like. There are totally author-itative Web sites on everything from begonia to baobob trees. There are chat rooms where you can ask questions—even really dumb ones, and the experts love to help and aren't condescend-ing. There is, as is usual with the 'Net, such an overwhelming amount of information that your eyes will start to cross after a while, and of course you'll find conflicting opinions. Even if you never become a rabid garden soldier, it's really fun to dip into these secret little worlds that you never knew existed, where a guy in the Czech Republic wants to send you some cactus cuttings or a frantic mother in Minnesota wants to save her daughter's second grade plant project, which was doing fine for four years until she repotted it last month. So even if you're barely machine-oriented like me, just give it a try. It's a benign way to get your feet wet—much better than playing one of those bloody medieval jousting games that people get hooked on, or going into weird chat rooms where you might get stalked.

The following is a selective and definitely not all-inclusive list of Web sites you should find interesting, and they will lead you to other Web sites, and on and on.

arizonacactus.com
>   (Just what it sounds like.)

begonias.com
>   Cloudy Valley Nursery (Everything about begonias.)

begonias.org
>   American Begonia Society

botany.com
>   (Extensive list of botanical and common plant names; how to cultivate numerous plants.)

cactus-mall.com
>   (Multilingual site including carnivorous cactus, the Hungarian Cactus Society, and everything in between.)

cssainc.org/index.html
>   Cactus and Succulent Society of America (Provides useful information and links to many other sites.)

daylilies.org
>   (Just what it sounds like.)

echonet.org

(Cookbook for Moringa; Web site for fighting world hunger using native tropical plants.)

freeplants.com

(Web site of Mike McGroarty of Ohio, a professional gardener who offers good propagation info for the northeast.)

garden.com

(Landscape software and plant finder.)

garden.org

National Gardening Association (Exhaustive general information and many links.)

gardenweb.com

(A plant database, plant exchanges, types of gardens.)

graylab.ac.uk/usr/hodgkiss/crecipe.html

(Lots of prickly pear paddle recipes from someone in the United Kingdom who can't even buy them there!)

hildnatives.com

Hild Nurseries (Large list of plants for prairie gardens and wetlands of the midwest.)

homeofclematis.com

(Just what it sounds like.)

iloveplants.com

(Gardeners Guide to the Internet)

io.com/neighbor/deerctrol.html

(Links to nuisance animal control.)

lithops.net

(For a huge variety of cactus and succulents.)

mdflora.org

Maryland Native Plant Society

met.police.uk/police/mps/mps/cprevent/garden.htm

(Scotland Yard's Web site for stolen plants, called Operation Bumblebee, with a list of unpleasantly thorny bushes you can plant to keep out burglars.)

newfs.org
  New England Wild Flower Society (the oldest one in the
  United States)
nhm.ac.uk/science/projects/fff/intro.htm.
  (England's Postcode plant database, important source or list
  of native plants and urgent need for their propagation and
  preservation.)
noble.org/imagegallery
  Noble Foundation Plant Image Gallery—Oklahoma, Texas
  (For information on wildflowers.)
palm.com
  (Everything you'll ever want to know about palms.)
prairienursery.com
  Prairie Nursery, Inc. (Very informative on prairie gardens
  for the midwest and general information for native gardens.)
seedman.com
  (For Moringa and all sorts of other unusual and exotic seeds.)
smgrowers.com/deer.htm
  (Plants that deer don't like; a list of hundreds.)
trees–seeds.com
  (A nursery that sells hard-to-get seeds for containers or garden, but also a great list of other gardening Web sites.)
vg.com
  (Basic gardening advice.)
web.ukonline.co.uk/alpines
  The Alpine Garden Rock Gardening on the 'Net
  (Comprehensive site on making and planting the basic alpine
  garden.)
westendnursery.com/plants
  (Flora for warm climates.)

RECOMMENDED READING

For quiet-time reading in the barracks . . .

Benton, Mike. *White Trash Gardening.* Dallas: Taylor Publishing Co., 1996.

Blackburne-Maze, Peter. *Propagation.* Surrey, England: Coombe Books, Quadrillion Publishing Ltd., 1999.

Downham, Fred. *Plant Propagation.* London: Ward Lock Master Gardener, 1993.

Efraimsson, Rulf. *65 Houseplants from Seeds, Pits and Kernels.* Santa Barbara, CA: Woodbridge Press Publishing Co., 1977.

Fitz, Franklin Herman. *A Gardener's Guide to Propagating Food Plants.* New York: Charles Scribners and Sons, 1983.

Halpin, Ann Moyer. *Foolproof Planting I.* Emmaus, PA: Rodale Press, 1990.

Hart, Rhonda Massingham. *Dirt Cheap Gardening.* Pownal, VT: Storey Communications, Inc., 1995.

Toogood, Alan. *Plant Propagation Made Easy.* Portland, OR: Timber Press, 1994.

Toogood, Alan, ed., *Plant Propagation.* New York: American Horticultural Society, DK Publishing, Inc., 1999.

barbara pallenberg's passion for gardening is matched only by her passion for modern art. The former vice president of the Impressionist and Modern paintings department for Sotheby's, she served for twenty years as an expert appraiser for the world's leading auctioneer.

Between 1983 and 1992, Pallenberg was the on-air commentator regarding the art market for the *Financial News Network*. Today, she conducts a busy lecture series throughout the western United States on evaluating, buying, and selling art at auctions. Pallenberg is a frequent contributor to art and design magazines. This is her first gardening book.